CHECKERED FLAG COOKING

An Insider's Guide to Tailgating at the Races

CHECKERED FLAG COOKING

An Insider's Guide to Tailgating at the Races

Kent "The Deck Chef" Whitaker

QUAIL RIDGE PRESS

Preserving America's Food Heritage

Library of Congress Cataloging-in-Publication Data

Whitaker, Kent, 1965-
Checkered flag cooking : an insider's guide to tailgating at the races / Kent "The Deck Chef" Whitaker.
p. cm.
Includes index.
ISBN-10: 1-893062-76-7
ISBN-13: 978-1-893062-76-4
1. Outdoor cookery. 2. Tailgate parties 3. Automobile racing I. Title.

TX823.W46 2005
641.5'78 —dc22 2005007735

ISBN-10: 1-893062-76-7
ISBN-13: 978-1-893062-76-4

Cover photos shot on location by Allyson Whitaker at Hixson Motorsports, Soddy Daisy, Tennessee. Front cover food prepared by the race fans and fantastic pitmasters at Spencer B's Barbecue in Ringgold, Georgia, and Chattanooga, Tennessee. Back cover food by Kent Whitaker.

Design by Cynthia Clark.
Printed in Canada

First edition

Quail Ridge Press
P. O. Box 123 • Brandon, MS 39043 • 1-800-343-1583
email: info@quailridge.com • www.quailridge.com

DEDICATION

This book is dedicated to my son Macee Whitaker. Seeing the light in his eyes and the grin on his face when he heard the most famous words in racing—"Gentlemen, start your engines!" for the first time is a memory that a proud father will never forget. When we left the pit area after his first race, Macee said, "Dad, I think that was the best time I have ever had. Thank you." Those are words a father holds dear to his heart and they can never, ever be taken away. I got a great big hug that day.

This book is also dedicated to the Original Grill Master Jake. I will forever miss my four-legged buddy. Please support animal rescue.

This book is also dedicated to my wife Ally and her dog Barney. Starting up the grill and grabbing some peanuts has never been so much fun! Thank you for being much, much better than a dream.

If you can't catch a race from the living room . . . or from the stands . . . or from the campgrounds and tailgate areas . . . then the next best place must be on top of one of the race team's carhaulers in the garage and pit area. From left to right: Kent, Macee and Ally Whitaker.

Jake Says—

Before any tailgate at the track, check to see what kind of outdoor cooking is allowed. Make sure you can fire up your ultimate tailgate grill or smoker.

TABLE OF CONTENTS

PREFACE

I have high hopes for this new cookbook. Sheila, my editor and publisher, and now trusted friend, asked me what I wanted to write about after my *Smoke in the Mountains Cookbook.* I blurted out racing and cooking. "OK, go for it," was her reply.

The great thing about auto racing is the fact that not only are there great cars, drivers, tracks and stories involved, but there is also great FOOD! I am always on the hunt for recipes that I can cook on the grill. Much of this translates to foods that can be cooked during a tailgate party. Talking to people at the track has other advantages—I always make good friends and hear a great story or two.

From small dirt ovals around the country to the huge superspeedways, a common thing is delicious food and fun people. From the fans, to the track restaurants, to the camper cities at the big races, great food can always be found!

It is an idea I have been thinking about for years. Why not combine two of the things I enjoy most—racing and food? Every weekend, from large tracks to small dirt ovals, people gather to race or watch a race. Today people of all ages, races and sex enjoy and participate in the sport. Inside and outside of tracks, teams and fans are grilling and cooking.

Tracks often hire caterers and chefs to feed hungry crowds and VIPs. Many teams in larger series such as NASCAR actually hire their own team chefs to cater their meals. Even in the smaller series, on any given race day, you can walk along the line of car-haulers and find somebody designated as the "team chef." They will be cooking on a hot grill for a hungry crew. Maybe it's the truck driver, or the driver's mom, or his wife . . . any member of the crew who can cook something that tastes good!

The recipes in this book have been credited to the generous people who have offered some of their favorite trackside creations. All recipes that don't have a credit are my own personal favorites.

I have been lucky enough to find a great resource in the form of my friend, Fiona. She knows a ton about racing from a fan's point of view, as well as being involved with the sport as a former PR director for a race team. When I told her my idea, true to Fiona-form, she started to break the idea down into workable tasks.

Over the course of writing this book, I traveled to many tracks and races. I met many wonderful people along the way. A great thing about writing this cookbook was that I sampled tons of food. Two days before a race, I was in the RV area meeting and greeting drivers and teams; many of them were cooking out. Let's see, the average is about forty-three teams per field. That's about thirty teams I met . . . twenty dinners I ate . . . and one hundred side dishes and snacks I tasted! I learned to pace myself.

This book was written as a fun guide to cooking and eating around a sport I love—stock car racing. All of the teams, tracks, series and other businesses and individuals listed or mentioned in the book are as up-to-date as possible. However, due to the rapidly changing world of motorsports, things may change—some teams may be gone, some drivers may have retired or switched teams and some track information may have changed.

This book is not only about cooking and such in the garage area and pits. I have tried to make it more than that. I have included profiles and bios on people and places from NASCAR to the local dirt tracks, from drivers to crew members, officials and fans. That, combined with some fun tailgate tips, and track, series and campground info, makes for a good read. Oh, did I mention the GREAT recipes from drivers, teams, fans and more? Cooking, eating and talking a good story—that's what I do best!

Well, here we go behind the pace car into the world of motorsports and cooking. Like Scott Borchetta, Nashville NASCAR Truck Weekly Series driver and Nashville music executive, told my son, "Go fast and turn left!" Keep turning these pages, enjoy the ride and LET'S GET COOKING!

And now to paraphrase the most famous words in motorsports . . .

TAILGATERS . . . START YOUR ENGINES!

SPECIAL THANKS

- Special thanks to all of the drivers, teams, tracks, sponsors and PR and media reps in all of the racing series I visited. Thanks to all of the race fans, chefs, campground chefs and everyone else who loved sitting down, or standing up around a grill, and talking about swapping paint and food!
- Thanks to Mom, Dad, my brothers Ty and Scot, Tonya and all of my nieces.
- Thanks to Fiona Lynn Shaffer.
- Thanks to Hixson Motorsports and the entire #23 ARCA RE/MAX team.
- Thanks to Coulter Racing and the #4 SAS racing team and KC Racing Graphics.
- Thanks to ARCA, ASA, SAS, USAR Hooters Pro Cup, BUSCH NASCAR and Weekly Series, and all of their representatives.
- Thanks to all of the tracks from the superspeedways to the local dirt tracks.
- Thanks to Big Tom Price and Fred of John Boy and Billy and everyone at bigshowfoods.com.
- A special thanks to Sheila "Harley" Simmons, my editor, publisher and friend for keeping my head above water, and thanks to everyone else at Quail Ridge Press.
- Big thanks to Wes, Kat, Logan, Ashton. GO VOLS! God bless Joe's mom. In fact . . . thanks to all of my family and friends.
- Once again, thanks to Linda Terry Hickam and Homer Hickam . . . long story, but thanks!
- Thanks to all of the great people I met along the way.
- Thanks to Tennessee Valley Golden Retriever Rescue: www.tvgrr.com.

THE STARTING GRID

From the tailgates of the racing world, one thing can be said: Somewhere, somehow, great food will be on hand! Tailgating is tailgating—no matter where you are or what sport you are tailgating. The only difference is that race fans tend to tailgate for almost a week for one race on the BUSCH and NEXTEL Cup Series. That's more than a tailgate . . . that's a lifestyle! Even on the smaller series such as ARCA RE/MAX, ASA, SAS and weekly racing at local tracks across the country, somebody is cooking on a grill!

Top Ten Tailgate Main Dishes

These foods were listed by my buddies around the racing world as their favorites. The most popular things mentioned were burgers and dogs, mostly for cost and ease of cooking. But after that, the sky was the limit. Here is the very unofficial list of the top ten tailgating favorites! These all apply to the grill or smoker.

1. Huge hamburgers
2. Grilled franks, dogs, weiners
3. Ribs: pork or beef
4. Grilled chicken: wings, thighs, or breasts
5. Barbecue: pulled or shredded
6. Beer can chicken
7. A big steak
8. Smoked turkey: whole or legs
9. Brisket
10. Brats, smoked sausage

Kent's Tailgate Tips

Here is a quick list of tips and tricks you can use to keep your next tailgate fun, easy, interesting and safe.

- **Don't forget the water!** Sure, many people load up on everything else, but forget the basics, such as water, extra toilet paper, paper towels, etc.
- **Do some prep work before the party.** Plan your menu a few days or more before the race, and do your prep work before the race weekend, such as chopping vegetables or marinating meat. Freeze items, if possible.
- **Making a race-day checklist is a must.** Heck, even I admit I forget stuff.
- **Toss it, if possible.** Use paper plates, plastic forks, knives, cups, etc. That also means pick up your trash. Every campground has designated trash bins.
- **Bring lots of garbage bags.**
- **Always check the rules** for open flames and outdoor cooking at the campground where you are staying.
- **Don't forget the extra condiments.** A perfect time to use those leftover sauce packs from fast-food places. I have one friend who stops by his local restaurant supply store for cases of ketchup, barbecue, mustard and relish packets every season.
- **Bring a well-stocked first-aid kit.** Include burn spray, sun screen and headache medicine. If you are like me, a few sinus pills are in order as well.
- **Bring a grill thermometer.**
- **Always plan on using several coolers**—one for fresh ice and drinks, one for prepared items, veggies and condiments and a separate cooler for meats.
- **Camping tables, chairs, dining covers and tarps** are always nice to have.
- **Never forget your rain gear:** ponchos, rain coats, etc.
- **Bring a radio,** some CD's, batteries and extension cords.

- **Show your TEAM COLORS and NUMBERS!**
- **Always wash your hands.** Gloves and cleaning hand wipes are easy to pick up at many stores and restaurant supply shops.
- **Avoid contact between raw and cooked foods.**
- **Dishcloths should be rinsed in a bleach water solution:** one cup of bleach to two gallons of water.
- **Do not leave cooked foods out at room temperature** for more than two hours. If it is a hot day, such as above 90 degrees, don't leave food out for more than an hour.
- **Keep coolers out of direct sunlight.**
- **Cook foods to the proper internal temperature:** beef–170°; ground beef–160°; poultry–180°; ground poultry–165°.
- **Avoid cooking frozen meats.** Always thaw your meat in the fridge, not on the counter or outside.
- **Marinated foods should be marinated in the fridge.**
- **Leftover marinade,** after used on meat, should be tossed out. Or, cook it into a sauce by bringing the marinade to a boil for several minutes to destroy any possible bacteria and germs.
- **Use separate serving utensils** when serving food, or clean the utensils you cooked with.
- **If you are looking for a nice way to store** all of your cooking utensils, then use this great tip from my friends at Michigan International Speedway. Store in a large, plastic tool box or even a tackle box with moveable dividers. You can find these in all sizes, shapes and colors. When your tailgate is over, simply remove all of the cooking tools, wash them, then wash the box with soap and a hose.

Michael Waltrip

Driver – NASCAR, BUSCH
www.michaelwaltrip.com

One of the nicest drivers you will ever have a chance to meet is Michael Waltrip. During his press conference after winning the Pepsi 300 at Nashville Superspeedway, Michael proceeded to tell a host of stories and insights about the race and racing in general. He had the press people laughing for hours.

Michael Waltrip takes home a one-of-a-kind Gibson Les Paul guitar designed by motorsports artist, Sam Bass, after winning the Pepsi 300 at Nashville Superspeedway.

Michael Waltrip captured the Daytona 500 crown in 2001 and 2003, has competed for over sixteen seasons, and is well known to fans as being a great husband and father. "I want to thank my family, my wife and kids, and of course this great #99 Aaron's Dream Machine crew." Besides being a fantastic driver on the NEXTEL and BUSCH Series, almost every fan sees Waltrip as one of the "good guys" in the sport.

He is also one of the funniest drivers and can often use his faith to describe events on the track. "When all of those cars in front of me started wrecking and the track filled up with smoke, I just gritted my teeth and drove through it like the sea was parting! Next thing you know, all of them cars in front of me were gone!"

NEAT THINGS: Michael ran the Boston Marathon and the Tampa Marathon in 2000. In 2002 he was an Olympic Torch Bearer for the Salt Lake City Olympics. Michael was the first driver to honor Alan Kulwicki with a "Polish" victory lap after winning at Bristol in 1993.

QUALIFYING

There are many things that make for a great tailgate. One thing that sets tailgating at the races apart from other sports is the amount of time at the track. Heck, you could find yourself at a racetrack for up to four days depending on the race or series. So instead of just a pregame meal, race-day tailgaters have to add other menu items such as a complete breakfast. This section is your race weekend ticket to good breakfast foods, some fantastic ice cold beverages and a few other things. These are all designed to help you get ready for the big event one dish at a time. Hope you enjoy these quailifying dishes!

- ***Breakfast***
- ***Beverages***
- ***Appetizers***
- ***Dips and Salsas***

BREAKFAST

Homemade Blueberry Pancakes

2 cups self-rising flour
3 tablespoons sugar
2 cups milk
½ cup frozen blueberries
1 large egg
2 tablespoons oil

Mix well, adding more flour or milk, as needed, to make a batter that pours freely from a spoon. Cook over a hot griddle. Turn when bubbles form in pancake, and cook a little longer, until set. Turn as little as possible.

Submitted by Bill "Big Bill" Newsom – NASCAR / NHRA race fan

Apple Pancakes

A great race-day breakfast that combines only a few ingredients for some great taste.

3 cups pancake mix
1 (21-ounce) can apple pie filling
Water or milk as directed by box
Butter

Mix the pancake mix and pie filling together. According to Martin, he likes to break the big pieces of apple down with a fork. Slowly stir in the milk or water. You may not need as much, depending on how runny your pie filling is. If you add too much water and your batter gets too runny, just add a bit more mix. Cook in a large skillet, using butter as needed to keep pancakes from sticking. Turn when bubbles form in pancake. Cook on that side about a minute, then serve with your favorite topping.

Submitted by Martin L. – Jasper, TN – Bristol fan

Tailgate Tater Pancakes

2 cups self-rising flour
1 cup instant potatoes
3 eggs, beaten
$\frac{1}{4}$ cup sugar
$1\frac{2}{3}$ cups milk
$\frac{1}{4}$ cup oil

Combine all of the ingredients in a large bowl. Mix completely and add more milk if needed. Cook as you would regular pancakes, in a large skillet, using butter as needed to keep pancakes from sticking. Turn when bubbles form in pancake. Cook on that side about a minute, then serve with your favorite topping.

Note: You may also cook this batter in your nonstick waffle iron for a delicious tater waffle.

Jake Says—

Don't have a griddle handy? Don't worry. Fire up the grill, cover the cooking area with heavy-duty foil; when hot, cook your pancakes as usual.

Sausage Pancakes or Muffins

1 pound breakfast sausage
Pancake batter for about 2 dozen pancakes

This is a neat recipe. I have shown it to several tailgate buddies who now enjoy making it, too. Simply brown the sausage, drain, crumple into small pieces and mix in with your pancake batter. Cook like pancakes, and serve hot. Another idea is to pre-cook the batter in paper muffin cups in a 350° oven, 15–20 minutes. Chill, save and reheat the morning of the race. Top with butter and syrup, and eat!

Corn Bread Pancakes

1½ cups self-rising yellow cornmeal
1 cup self-rising flour
2 cups milk
½ stick butter, melted
2 tablespoons maple syrup
1 teaspoon sugar
2 large eggs

Combine everything and mix well. Cook in a large skillet, using butter as needed to keep pancake from sticking. Turn when bubbles form in pancake. Cook on that side about a minute longer.

Submitted by Martin L. – Jasper, TN – Bristol fan

Chocolate Waffles

Looking for a neat idea to keep the kids happy during breakfast? Get a box of instant pancake mix and some chocolate syrup for a simple and quick cooking idea that makes for a different twist on a waffle.

⅓ cup chocolate syrup
¼ cup oil
1 teaspoon vanilla
2 cups instant pancake mix
1 egg (or as directed on box)
Milk or water as needed per box
2 tablespoons sugar

Combine ingredients, and cook in nonstick waffle iron till done. You can also try this using butterscotch or strawberry syrup.

First Baptist Church National Corn Bread Waffles

If you ever get a chance to visit the National Corn bread Festival in South Pittsburgh, Tennessee, do it. The small town of South Pittsburgh, about 35 minutes from Chattanooga, swells in size for one weekend every April. Not only is great corn bread available, but you can also get many other wonderful foods. This recipe was given to me by "A Closer Walk Sunday School Class." What a great idea for a different take on waffles!

1 cup flour
1 cup cornmeal
4 tablespoons brown sugar
2 teaspoons baking powder
½ teaspoon salt
2 eggs, beaten
1 cup milk
¼ cup oil
2 teaspoons vanilla flavoring

Mix all ingredients, and cook in nonstick waffle iron till done. This recipe makes about 10 normal-size waffles.

Submitted by "A Closer Walk Sunday School Class"
First Baptist Church, South Pittsburgh, TN

Kent is flanked by drivers Michael Ritch and Tom Buzz during a fan event in Jefferson, Georgia.

French Toast Waffles

This recipe was given to me by a race fan at one of the many events I visited while working on this book. It was written on the back of a card. It's so simple that I had to try it when I got home. Many thanks to the fan who suggested cooking French toast this way.

Your favorite recipe for French toast
Slices of white bread
Nonstick waffle iron
Syrup
Butter
Powdered sugar

Mix your French toast recipe. Dip bread in, and let excess drip off. Cook bread in a nonstick waffle iron. Remove, serve hot, and top with syrup, butter and powdered sugar.

Frozen Waffle French Toast

This idea actually came from camping around the Nashville area as a kid. It's the perfect addition to your file of quick breakfast tailgate items.

3 eggs, beaten
⅓ cup milk
1 tablespoon sugar
1 tablespoon cinnamon
½ teaspoon brown sugar
1 (10-count) box frozen waffles

Combine all of the ingredients except the waffles in a bowl, and mix well. Dip each waffle in the egg mixture, and let soak for a bit on both sides. Cook as you would regular French toast (in a skillet with butter).

HEY RACE FANS, did you know that Jeff Gordon is the youngest driver to win at Dover at 24 years, 1 month and 13 days old?

Easy French Toast

Bill Newsom is a big guy. "They call me Big Bill." I met Bill during a race weekend when I was interviewing somebody else. Bill informed me that any book that deals with racing and cooking needed his French toast recipe. "What makes it special?" I asked. "I do. I'm special!" Bill said, with a huge smile. According to Bill, he has tailgated several races, countless football games and a few other things, and no matter what, he cooks his favorite Easy French Toast.

8 slices Texas toast
3 eggs, beaten
½ cup milk
1 tablespoon brown sugar
1 teaspoon cinnamon

Cut the toast in half. Mix remaining ingredients. Dip a piece of toast in egg/milk mixture, and fry in a skillet with butter. Stir ingredients after each piece of toast is dipped. Cook until golden brown and serve hot. "The secret is to stir after every piece to mix up the sugar and such," Bill said.

Submitted by Bill "Big Bill" Newsom – NASCAR / NHRA race fan

Honey Pecan French Toast

Ally can tell you this recipe is great . . . even if you forget to bring the pecans!

1 cup whole milk
5 large eggs, beaten
4 tablespoons honey
1 tablespoon cinnamon
½ cup finely minced pecans
1 teaspoon vanilla

Combine all of the ingredients and whisk well.

Bread slices
Butter

Continue to mix as you dip bread into the mix. You may need to add more cinnamon as you go. Cook the French toast over medium-hot heat with lots of butter until golden brown on each side.

Submitted by Alex – Dale, Jr. fan

Honey Butter

2 sticks butter
1 tablespoon cinnamon
1 cup honey

Melt butter in a saucepan. Combine with remaining ingredients and simmer for a few minutes. Serve warm.

Submitted by Sheri "The Chef" and Foster – BUSCH Series fans

Easy Apple Butterscotch Syrup

½ (12-ounce) bottle your favorite syrup
1 cup butterscotch ice cream syrup
½ cup apple juice
Cinnamon (optional)

Combine all of the ingredients, and warm through. You can use applesauce for a thicker sauce. It's great with some cinnamon tossed in.

Alex – Dale, Jr. fan

Orange Raspberry Syrup

2 cups rinsed raspberries
⅔ cup water
1 tablespoon lemon juice
1 tablespoon cinnamon
⅔ cup unsweetened orange juice

Crush raspberries with a fork, if desired. Mix with water, lemon juice and cinnamon in a saucepan. Simmer and stir in orange juice. Serve warm.

Orange Maple Syrup

1 (12-ounce) bottle maple syrup
1 cup orange juice
2 tablespoons melted butter

Mix and warm before serving.

Submitted by Sheri "The Chef" and Foster – BUSCH Series fans

Peach Pancake Syrup

1 (16- to 20-ounce) package frozen peaches
1/2 cup maple syrup or corn syrup
1/3 cup sugar
1/3 cup water

Thaw peaches in a bowl, and reserve juice. Mash with a fork or blender. Combine with remaining ingredients in a large saucepan, and simmer. Serve hot over pancakes.

Submitted by Kevin and Jennifer – Race fans

Deck Chef Tip!

Gettin' fruity

Fresh fruit is great, but for tailgating, try a bag of frozen diced fruit. You can eat it thawed, or like my buddy Logan—he eats it still frozen right out of the bag.

Easy Breakfast Rice for a Crowd

This recipe will help feed your crew and a few buddies, too. According to Stephen, he cooks it beforehand at the house, freezes it and heats it up as needed. "I break it into four freezer bags and just heat it up at the track."

3 cups rice
6 cups water
2 sticks butter
2 beef buillon cubes
2 pounds sausage
Salt and pepper to taste
Parsley

Cook the rice in water, butter and buillon cubes. Bring to a boil. Reduce heat and simmer covered until rice is done. Keep moist. Cook the sausage and break into small pieces. Do not over-drain because you want the extra flavor from the grease. Combine all of the ingredients, and stir until mixed. Serve hot.

Submitted by Stephen C. – Memphis, TN – Race fan

Chunky Bacon Hash Browns

1 (16-ounce) bag frozen tater tots
1 ($10\frac{3}{4}$-ounce) can cream of mushroom soup
1 cup shredded mild Cheddar cheese
1 package bacon, cooked and crumbled
1 onion, diced
Salt and pepper to taste

Combine all of the ingredients, and place in a greased baking dish. Cook, uncovered, in a 350° oven for 30 minutes. Serve hot.

Submitted by Christy M. – Robby Gordon fan

HEY RACE FANS, did you know that Greg Biffle is the only driver to capture both the NASCAR Craftsman Truck Series and the NASCAR BUSCH Series Championship?

Christi Passmore

Driver – ARCA RE/MAX Series
www.christipassmoremotorsports.com

At the age of twelve Christi Passmore's father bought her a mini sprint and took it apart. "He told me that if I wanted to race, I would have to put the car back together and then talk my mom into letting me race." According to Christi, putting the car back together was the easier task.

Now you can find Christi tearing up racetracks in the ARCA Series. From superspeedways such as Talladega and Daytona to the short tracks along the circuit, Christi has made a mark with other drivers and fans. In the garage area, Christi's hauler is always popular because of the fantastic food produced by her great friend and designated team chef, Lu. "I try to feed these guys the best I can. I am very familiar with just about every grocery store along the series!" Lu says with a smile.

With all Christi has done in her racing life, she is most proud of one race. "Beating my dad for the first time at Mayetta, Kansas, in a sprint car."

NEAT THINGS: Favorite food is chicken • Favorite music is country • Her dogs are named Hoosier and Chassis • She drives her own HUGE motor home to every race.

Hash Brown Casserole

This recipe is great straight from the oven, heated up after being frozen, or even like I had it during the early races at the beginning of the year . . . out of the back of a carhauler served to freezing crew members on a foggy morning, heated up in a microwave and served in Styrofoam cups.

2 (10¾-ounce) cans cream of potato soup
1 cup sour cream
½ teaspoon garlic salt
Salt and pepper to taste
1 (2-pound) bag frozen hash browns
2 cups shredded Cheddar cheese
½ cup Parmesan cheese

Mix soup, sour cream and spices together. Stir in hash browns and Cheddar cheese. Place in greased casserole. Top with Parmesan cheese. Bake at 350° for 1 hour.

Submitted by Tony Taffar – Gasman/Cook
#16 Naturally Fresh USAR Hooters Pro Cup Series

Tater Breakfast

1 (16-ounce) bag frozen steak fries
Cajun seasoning
8–10 eggs
½ cup milk
1 cup shredded Cheddar cheese
1 package bacon, cooked and crumbled
½ cup diced onion
1 tablespoon minced garlic
Salt and pepper to taste

In a greased casserole dish, place the steak fries and top with Cajun seasoning. Bake at 350° about 20 minutes. While the taters are cooking, combine the remaining ingredients in a bowl and mix very well. Remove the taters from the oven and pour the egg mixture over; return to the oven to cook about 15 minutes. Top with some extra cheese, if desired.

Submitted by Bob H. – Tennessee – Dirt track fan / NASCAR fan

English Muffins Breakfast Pizzas

The English muffin is making a comeback. This bread is all over the place—during breakfast, lunch and dinner!

1 package English muffins
Your favorite mild salsa
4 eggs
Link sausage, diced
Shredded cheese

Open the English muffins, and separate the tops from the bottoms. Spread a layer of salsa over each muffin piece. Cook your eggs scrambled along with the sausage. Place equal amounts of eggs and sausage mix over each muffin piece, and top with cheese. Bake until cheese melts. Serve hot.

Submitted by M. A. – Mississippi – Dirt track wife

One-Dish Breakfast Casserole

1 pound bulk breakfast sausage
8 slices bread
8 eggs
1 cup cheese
1 cup milk

Cook and drain sausage. Tear bread into small pieces. Spread sausage in bottom of 9x13-inch casserole dish. Stir together eggs, bread, cheese and milk. Pour mixture over sausage, and place in refrigerator overnight.

Bake at 350° for 45 minutes. Try serving with applesauce and sliced tomatoes.

Submitted by Michigan International Speedway infield guest, Jim
Used with permission of MISpeedway

A great seat for a race! Team members, family and friends of drivers and teams often head to the top to their campers and trailers for a better view of the track from the infield garage area.

English Eggs Benedict

Yes, you can enjoy a good eggs Benedict at the track. This recipe is pretty standard and the Hollandaise Sauce is easy as well. It comes from a great race fan named Sheri whose hobby is cooking. So her tailgates, parties and Super Bowl munchy spreads are something to see!

1 package Canadian bacon
Butter
Water
Salt and pepper to taste
3 tablespoons white vinegar
8–9 eggs
4 English muffins
Parsley

Warm the slices of bacon in a little butter. Do not over-brown. In a large skillet, add enough water to cover the bottom about ½ inch deep, and add salt, pepper and vinegar. Stir and bring to a boil. Break each egg carefully into the water. Remove from water when the eggs are solid enough to lift with a spatula or large spoon. Place a slice of Canadian bacon on each muffin piece, and top with an egg, Hollandaise Sauce (see page 132) and parsley.

Dozen Campsite Scrambled Eggs

Sheri says if you don't feel like going through all of the trouble for some eggs Benedict, then just enjoy these fantastic campsite scrambled eggs. "Just toss a bunch of extra things in and people will love it!"

1 dozen large eggs, scrambled
1 small onion, chopped
1 cup crumbled cooked sausage
½ cup finely diced green pepper
¼ cup milk
1–2 tablespoons butter
1 cup shredded Cheddar cheese

Combine all of the ingredients except butter and cheese, and mix well. Cook in a very large nonstick pan over medium-low heat with some melted butter. Gently stir. Sheri offers this advice for eggs: "Do not overcook or cook over heat that is too high, or your eggs will get tough. Just before removing the eggs from the heat, stir in the cheese to melt it."

Submitted by Sheri "The Chef" and Foster – BUSCH Series fans

Zip-Close Messy Omelets

This is a great idea that I have seen at several races. Simply cook your omelet in a zip-close bag in boiling water!

1 teaspoon butter
2 eggs per omelet
2 slices ham, chopped
Chopped onion
Chopped peppers
¼ cup shredded Cheddar cheese

You can actually add any ingredients you would prefer to this omelet; I just listed some of my favorites! Scramble everything together and place in a heavy-duty, zip-close sandwich bag. Make sure the bag is properly closed, and place in a large pot of boiling water. This way you can cook several omelets at a time. Cook about 3–4 minutes, or until done to your liking.

Easy Breakfast Burrito

This great idea comes from Bill Robinson, a race fan who visits Michigan International Speedway.

Follow the directions for the Zip-Close Messy Omelets (above), but try Bill's twist. "We have a big pot for deep-frying turkeys and use it to heat water all weekend. Everyone makes their eggs and marks the bag with a marker. They can add whatever they want. When the eggs are set, dump on a warm tortilla, add salsa and fold."

Submitted by Michigan International Speedway infield guest, Bill Robinson – Used with permission of MISpeedway

Quiche and Toast

Real men do eat quiche and so do many race fans!

Bread slices
4 eggs, beaten
¼ cup milk
⅓ cup chopped onion
1½ cups shredded cheese
1 cup real bacon bits
Salt and pepper to taste
Garlic powder to taste

Coat a muffin pan with nonstick spray. Gently press a piece of bread into each muffin hole. Work slowly to avoid tearing the bread. Cook the bread in the oven at 350° about 5 minutes to set the shape. Mix remaining ingredients and spoon into each piece of toast; cook an additional 10–15 minutes or until top of quiche is golden. Serve hot. "This is a favorite with my wife and me. It's easy and tastes great."

Submitted by D. – ARCA RE/MAX pit row official

Deck Chef Tip!

Cheaper by the dozen

Eggs are easy and cheap to prepare at a race. Don't cook them at too high a temperature or they will become hard and chewy instead of light and fluffy. You can add everything from butter and cheese to meat and veggies and have a great meal!

Deluxe Grits

Grits
Chicken broth
Milk
Muenster Cheese
Salt and pepper to taste

Cook the grits according to package directions, but use chicken broth (and less liquid than normal) in place of water. As the grits cook and need more liquid, use milk in them. When the grits are done, add a block of Muenster cheese and stir it in good. Season to taste. (I use stone-ground grits because I think they are much better.)

Submitted by Tony Taffar – Gasman/Cook #16 Naturally Fresh USAR Hooters Pro Cup Series

Cheese Grits Casserole

2 cups water
1 chicken bouillon cube
½ cup beer
1 tablespoon minced garlic
½ teaspoon salt
⅔ cup grits
½ cup shredded Cheddar cheese
½ cup shredded pepper cheese
¼ cup grated Parmesan cheese
3 eggs, beaten
2 cups frozen hash browns
Salt and pepper to taste
Cheese of your choice, shredded

In a large saucepan, bring water to a boil, then add bouillon cube, beer, garlic, salt and grits. Boil 20–25 minutes. Do not allow the grits to stick or burn. Remove from heat and stir in all three cheeses.

In a bowl, combine grits mixture, beaten eggs, hash browns, salt and pepper. Place in a greased and floured 8x12-inch cake pan. Bake at 350° about 20 minutes. Top with cheese of your choice; return to oven until cheese melts.

Barry's Instant Grits

I have only met a few people making grits at the track. Almost everybody uses quick grits. And that's fine by me. The easier, the better is often a rule of thumb.

2 cups instant grits
Water as directed
½ chicken bullion cube
1 tablespoon milk
2 tablespoons butter

Combine all of the ingredients except the butter. Cook the grits per package instructions. When done, stir butter into hot grits. Serve hot.

Submitted by Barry Tims – NASCAR fan

Quick Sausage Gravy

1 pound bulk pork sausage
4 tablespoons flour
1½ cups skim milk
Salt and pepper to taste

In large skillet over medium-high heat, cook and crumble sausage till lightly browned, removing fat from pan as it accumulates. Sprinkle flour over sausage in skillet, and stir to blend; add milk to pan all at once. Cook, stirring constantly, over medium-high heat, until thickened and bubbly. Season to taste with salt and pepper. Serve over hot baked biscuits, toasted English muffins or toast.

Submitted by the National Pork Board, proud sponsor of Frank Kimmel,
5-time ARCA RE/MAX Series champion
#46 Advance Auto Parts Ford
www.otherwhitemeat.com

HEY RACE FANS, did you know that MIS (Michigan International Speedway) was the first track to use the Jet-Track dryer system?

Janet Guthrie

Driver – NASCAR
www.janetguthrie.com

I remember growing up in Louisville, Kentucky, where the racing news of the day was dominated by INDY style cars. Somewhere in the news I remembered this really cool lady I saw once that drove closed course, Indy cars, and even NASCAR. As a kid who liked racing I have remembered the name Janet Guthrie for years.

When I started this book, one of the first people I tried to contact was Janet. As I had hoped, she is as nice and helpful as I had always imagined her to be. "Back when I was racing in the Sports Car Club of America, before I got the chance to drive at Indianapolis and Daytona, all my crew were volunteers. We often camped out at the races. That made me the chief cook, as well as driver and chief mechanic. Often I would make spaghetti sauce with chopped beef from Craig Claiborne's first cookbook, *The New York Times Cook Book*, before leaving home, and put it in the ice chest, then cook the spaghetti on a Coleman stove."

When Janet and her crew moved up to Indy and NASCAR, that great food changed a bit. "After I got my chance at the top, my race-weekend cooking activities were usually limited to making sandwiches for the crew at lunchtime (since I wasn't driving for rich teams). It's sure different now, with the teams bringing motor homes and their own gourmet chefs!"

Achievements: NASCAR Winston Cup Official Rookie Season, 1977.
Neat things: Team owner: Lynda Ferreri; Sponsor: Kelly Girl; Car: Chevrolet Laguna

Camp Bacon and Cheese Spoon Biscuits

2⅓ cups Jiffy Baking Mix
⅔ cup water
½ cup shredded mild Cheddar
⅔ cup real bacon bits
½ cup butter, melted

Combine all of the ingredients, and mix well. Spoon onto nonstick surface, and bake about 20 minutes or until golden brown.

Submitted by Jerry S. – Florida – Father of go-kart racer family

Apple Biscuits

This is a quick recipe; I have seen similar versions at several races.

2 (10-count) cans flaky biscuits
Applesauce
Melted butter
Brown sugar

Open the biscuit cans, and separate each biscuit. Place a bit of applesauce in between the biscuit sections, and press back together. Cook in an oven as package directs, or wrap in foil and toss in hot coals for a few minutes. Before serving, brush with butter and sprinkle with brown sugar.

I have seen these cooked with nuts, fruit and jelly, and topped with icing. Try some of your favorite items and flavors.

Submitted by Alex – Dale, Jr. fan

HEY RACE FANS, did you know that driver Paul Menard completed the "ABC" during the 2003 racing season? That means he competed in ARCA RE/MAX, BUSCH Series and even the Craftsman Truck Series.

Big Cat-Head Biscuits

I've been making biscuits for a long time. Here is a recipe that really works well. Just double the ingredients for larger numbers of people. The trick to any decent biscuit is to not over-knead the dough. This way your biscuits don't come out flat, hard and thin.

2 cups flour
2 teaspoons baking powder
½ teaspoon baking soda
½ teaspoon salt
3 tablespoons cold butter, cut into bits
3 tablespoons shortening, cut into bits
¾ cup milk

Combine all of the ingredients, and gently mix. On a floured surface, knead the dough with your fingertips until it is consistent, but not too firm. Spread to an even thickness of about an inch, and cut with a large biscuit cutter.

Deck Chef Tip!

Better biscuits

- Always use cold butter and shortening.
- Work quickly.
- Do not over-knead.
- For crisp biscuits, brush with a bit of water before cooking.
- For soft biscuits, brush with a bit of milk before cooking.
- Use a biscuit cutter, not a glass or jar or old can. The sharp clean edge of a biscuit cutter makes a clean cut which allows a biscuit to rise. If you use a dull cutter such as a glass or a deviled ham can with a hole punched in the top, the edges will press or seal together which will make the biscuit edges harder to rise.

Side Dish Biscuits

2½ cups self-rising flour
2 tablespoons granulated sugar
1½ cups heavy (whipping) cream
2 tablespoons butter or margarine, melted
1 cup chopped ham
Additional melted butter

Combine all ingredients except additional melted butter. Gently knead, roll out onto a floured surface and cut into biscuits. Brush tops with butter, and cook at 350° until tops are golden brown.

Quick Chocolate-Topped Donuts

Oil
2 (10-count) cans instant biscuits
Powdered sugar
Cinnamon
1 (16-ounce) container chocolate cake frosting

Heat your oil in a deep saucepan. Drop only a few biscuits into the oil at a time. Fry until puffy and brown. Remove from oil and roll in sugar and cinnamon. Top with a bit of chocolate frosting. Serve hot.

Breakfast Trail Mix

According to Susan, this is a lifesaver and makes for a quick breakfast, munchie food, late night snack or whatever. And it's pretty simple, considering you only have to buy two ingredients!

1 multi-pack breakfast cereal
1 (12-ounce) box raisins

Buy a pack of individual cereal boxes and a box of raisins. Open all of the boxes and mix in a large freezer bag. Serve whenever anybody wants a morning snack.

Submitted by Susan and Robert – Short track nuts

BEVERAGES

Banana Rama Smoothie

A great recipe adapted from a recipe card given to me while I waited in line buying tailgate supplies at a supermarket. Of course I made some race-day adjustments!

3 bananas
1 cup yogurt, your favorite flavor
¼ cup piña colada mix (optional)
2 tablespoons honey
¼ tablespoon cinnamon
30 large ice cubes

Combine everything except ice cubes in a blender, and blend until smooth. Slowly add in the ice and continue to blend. Serves 4–5.

Piña Colada Smoothie

Liquid piña colada mix
2 bananas
Strawberries
Vanilla ice cream
Ice
Coconut
Water as needed

Slice the bananas; clean the strawberries. In a blender, pour about a cup or more of piña colada mix; toss in some bananas, strawberries, ice cream, some coconut, ice and a few spoons of water. Hit the button and enjoy.

Scott's Famous Punch

Scott is a die-hard NASCAR fan. "I love the sound they make when they come around for a green flag start." When we talked about camping and tailgating, he said he really enjoyed Atlanta, had fun in Nashville and Talledega, but nothing beats Speedweek in Daytona. I asked him for a recipe and he said his favorite was actually a punch recipe. If you ask him why it's famous, he will tell you that's because it sounds better than just "punch."

2 (6-ounce) cans frozen lime concentrate
1 (6-ounce) can frozen orange juice concentrate
1 (2-liter) bottle ginger ale
1 bottle sparkly, fruity champagne
Ice

Mix all together; pour over ice or blend in a blender.

Submitted by Scott M. – Alabama – Richard Petty fan

How is this for a perfect tailgate item? A gas powered blender!!!

APPETIZERS

Campfire Fondue

Hey, it's fondue! What good is a cookbook without a neat fondue idea in it?

1 (10¾-ounce) can cream of mushroom soup (or cream of chicken)
½ cup beer or white wine
2 cups shredded Swiss cheese
2 tablespoons flour
¼ teaspoon paprika

Mix all of the ingredients together and cook over low heat until cheese is melted. Serve fondue style with bread pieces.

Submitted by Michigan International Speedway campground guest, Sue
Used with permission of MISpeedway

Sarah's Celery Sticks

Joe's mom is a great lady. Being able to survive the childhood of one of the funniest Bill Elliot fans I have ever met says a bunch! Here are her easy and great-tasting celery sticks—a snack I truly enjoy!

1 package celery stalks
1 small sweet onion
1 block extra sharp Cheddar cheese

Clean and rinse the celery. Cut into 2-inch pieces. Mince the onion and grate the cheese. Mix until you have a paste. Fill the celery sticks with the mix, and serve.

Note: This recipe works great with crackers as well. Of course you know I had to mess with the recipe a bit. I added some cream cheese, some imitation crabmeat and chili powder.

Submitted by Sarah Norman – Mother of a Bill Elliot fan

Cheese Pretzels

I tried these in North Carolina. They were made beforehand and allowed to cool, then placed in a zip-close bag. According to the nice people who let me try a few, you can use any cheese you want and add the seasoning of your choice.

1 bag pretzels
½ cup shredded Cheddar cheese
½ cup shredded pepper cheese
1 tablespoon seasoned salt

Spread the pretzels over a nonstick cookie sheet. Combine the cheeses, and carefully sprinkle each pretzel with some cheese. Then sprinkle the pretzels with the seasoned salt. Bake in a 300° oven about 5 minutes or until cheese melts. Allow to cool if placing in a container for later. If not, serve hot.

Deck Chef Tip!

No time for that!

Snacks are a staple at tailgate parties. If you don't have the time or equipment to make your own from scratch, then don't worry about it. Just stock up on packaged cookies, fruit cups, chips and such. Store them all in a large plastic storage container. Label it SNACKS!

Cajun Mixed Peanuts

According to LeeAnn, this recipe was one her dad used to make for every sporting event they watched. "When my husband and I went overnight to Bristol with some friends, I was in charge of snacks and stuff. This was the first thing I put on the list. They were a big hit with everybody."

2 (11-ounce) cans mixed nuts
⅓ cup oil
⅓ cup olive oil
¼ cup Cajun seasoning
2 cups mini pretzels
2 cups oyster crackers
Chili powder
Garlic powder

Put the nuts into a large skillet and warm with the oils. Add the Cajun seasoning and stir until well coated. Allow as much of the oil to cook off as possible. Cool for a few minutes, then pour the nuts into a bowl, and slowly stir in the pretzels and crackers. Sprinkle with chili powder and garlic powder, as desired. "Serve the same day, if possible, because the pretzels and oyster crackers won't last too long!"

Submitted by LeeAnn – Dawsonville, GA – Bill Elliot fan

Mini Pizzas

A nice snack that you can make in an oven or covered grill. Thanks to Ed and his family for the suggestion. They did this at a birthday party for their child, then tried it at the track the night before a race. "We did it buffet style and the whole gang enjoyed it."

2 (10-count) cans biscuits
1 (14-ounce) jar pizza sauce
Shredded cheese
Assorted toppings

Open the cans and press the biscuits flat, but not too thin. Using a glass or cup, press down in the center to form an indention on the inside and an outer crust. Use as many different toppings as you like. "We have bowls set up with meats, veggies, mini shrimp, the sauce and the cheese. Everybody makes them how they like them." Cook in the oven (per can instructions) or covered grill until crust is golden brown.

Randy's Kielbasa Chunks

3 pounds kielbasa
Oil
Beer
1 (20-ounce) can pineapple chunks
½ cup brown sugar

Dice the kielbasa into small chunks. Brown with some oil in a frying pan. Add a bit of beer and a can of pineapple and the brown sugar. Simmer until the juice cooks off. Serve hot.

Submitted by Randy

Smoked Sausage Bites

Easy and quick! Make 'em before the big event and store in a zip-close bag.

12 hot dog-size smoked sausages
1 cup apple jelly
¼ cup ketchup
1 tablespoon yellow mustard
1 dash of garlic
Hot sauce to taste

Cut the sausages into 4 pieces each. Mix with remaining ingredients and store in a zip-close bag. Cook on skewers over a grill at the tailgate, or double the recipe and cook in a crockpot for indoor parties.

Brothers Jeff Green, Mark Green and David Green are all NASCAR-seasoned drivers. David and Jeff are the only two siblings to win the NASCAR BUSCH Series Crown.

Cheese and Sausage Bites

1 pound breakfast sausage
2 cups biscuit mix
½ cup shredded pepper cheese
½ cup shredded Cheddar cheese
1 egg

Mix all together and form into small balls. Cook on baking pans in 400° oven 12–15 minutes or until done.

Submitted by M. P. S. – Boone, NC – Short track fanatic

Sassy Sausage Roll-Ups

½ pound bulk sausage
1 (8-ounce) package cream cheese, softened
¼ cup John Boy and Billy's Grillin' Sauce
12 slices white bread, crust removed and cut in half
12 slices premium bacon, cut in half

In a frying pan, cook sausage; drain and crumble. Mix with cream cheese and John Boy and Billy's Grillin' Sauce. Spread each rectangle of bread with the sausage and cheese mixture. Roll them up and wrap with a slice of bacon. Secure with a toothpick, and bake for 15 minutes in a 350° oven.

Used with permission of Big Tom Price
www.bigshowfoods.com

Doggie Bites

This is a fun version of the old hot dogs simmered in barbecue sauce. I tried this recipe during a tailgate session at one of the many tracks I visited and didn't write it down, or even who it came from or exactly what was in it. So I tried it at home and came up with my own version. That's the great thing about camper cities at racetracks—they're full of fun and great ideas.

1 package hot dogs
½ pound smoked sausage
½ pound kielbasa
½ pound bratwurst
½ pound frozen meatballs
1 can sloppy joe mix
2 cups favorite barbecue sauce
Water as needed

Slice all of the meats into bite-size pieces. Combine with everything else in a crockpot. Simmer for as long as possible and serve hot. If you have a favorite meat . . . toss it in! Store in a freezer bag until needed at your track event, then just warm them up!

Jake Says—

Buy precooked sausage and pancakes from the freezer section. Heat 'em, roll 'em into a soft taco shape, and dip 'em in maple syrup.

Kent's Corn Dog Bites

My son and I have learned how to make great corn dogs. The secret is to cut each hot dog or brat into thirds, coat with a very light layer of flour, then coat with your batter and fry as quickly as possible. We use a tabletop fryer, but skillets work just as well.

1 cup self-rising cornmeal
½ cup self-rising flour
1 (16-ounce) can creamed corn
½ cup shredded Cheddar cheese
¼ cup milk
¼ cup sugar
2 tablespoons Cajun seasoning
12 hot dogs, or 10 brats, cut into thirds, coated with flour
Several wooden skewers

Mix all ingredients except dogs or brats, and stir well. Place a bit of dog on the skewer. Dip in your mix and place quickly in the hot oil. Work quickly and spin the corn dog as it hits the oil for a few seconds before letting go. After a few minutes, you can push the dog off the skewer and reuse the skewer. Cook until golden brown. Serve hot. If your batter is too thick, just add a bit of milk.

Spicy Corn Dogs

An easy recipe to dress up frozen corn dogs.

1 large box frozen corn dogs
Melted butter
Lots of Cajun seasoning

Thaw the corn dogs, then baste with some butter and tons of Cajun seasoning. Grill them or cook them in a large foil pan.

Submitted by M. P. S. – Boone, NC – Short track fanatic

Hunter Robbins

SAS Driver #18 ATCO Chevrolet
www.hunterrobbinsracing.com

Hunter Robbins started racing at the age of six. "Both Greg and I raced so it was a natural that Hunter wanted to try it," Donna Robbins said of her son. According to Donna, they bought Hunter a nice store-bought go-kart and headed to a local track. "He was not impressed. His first words after the race were that it did not go fast enough!" So before the end of the night, they had bought a real racing kart. "Once we were going to go to a different series of cars where the door opened on the car. Hunter said if you didn't have to climb through the window, then it wasn't racing!" Donna said with a smile.

At thirteen, Hunter is a straight A student, a National Champ Racing Bandit and running third in points at his home track in Montgomery, Alabama, behind seasoned drivers. But Hunter is well grounded in what it takes to be a racer. "My friends think it is cool! But it is a lot of hard work. And we travel all of the time to the tracks." From Alabama to Tennessee, Florida to North Carolina, this racing family is always on the go during the summer following the SAS Series and other events. "It's a family affair," according to Hunter's mom.

NEAT THINGS: "I LOVE Mexican food and cheese dip! I love driving these stock cars with more horsepower. Besides racing, I want to play football for my school."

Bristol Beef Bites

A great pre-race snack. Requires a bit of work, but it is sure to take the checkered flag at your next race-day party! This recipe gets its name from the fact that the race fan who gave it to me is a Bristol short track nut!

½ pound ground beef, browned
1 tablespoon minced garlic
1 tablespoon bourbon
1 pat butter (about 1½ tablespoons)
¼ cup cream cheese, softened
¼ cup shredded Swiss cheese
¼ cup salsa
1 (8-count) can croissants

Brown ground beef. In a bowl, mix beef with garlic, bourbon, butter, cream cheese, Swiss cheese and salsa. Mix well. Cut each croissant in half. Fill with a spoonful of meat mix. Fold dough over and pinch shut. Cook in 350° oven until golden brown. Makes 16.

Speedway Cheese Ball

According to Daniel and Susan, nothing beats their Speedway Cheese Ball for a great snack item at their camper. "It's easy, tastes good and you can use it with crackers, veggies or as a sandwich spread," Susan said. Here is their recipe. Mind ya, it may be a bit hot for some!

2 (8-ounce) packages cream cheese
½ cup real bacon bits
½ cup shredded Jack cheese
¼ cup minced jalapeño peppers
1 tablespoon steak sauce
1 tablespoon hot sauce
1 tablespoon minced garlic
1 tablespoon parsley
⅓ cup finely chopped pecans

Soften the cream cheese. Combine all of the ingredients except the pecans. Mix well and form into a ball. You can add more shredded cheese if it is too mushy. Wrap tight in cling wrap and chill. Before serving, roll the cheese ball in the pecans and firmly press them into the ball. "I have come back and sprinkled it with Soul seasoning as well," Susan said.

Submitted by Daniel and Susan – Virginia
Jimmy Spencer / Dale, Jr. fans

Daniel raced motorcycles for years. "Now I just ride them . . . slow."

Cajun Cheese Cubes

A very simple way to serve up pieces of cheese!

1 block of your favorite cheese
1 tablespoon olive oil
1 tablespoon Cajun seasoning

Cube the cheese into small ½-inch pieces. Place in a zip-close bag and pour in the olive oil. Close the bag and toss gently until every piece has a light coating of oil. Mix in Cajun seasoning, adding more if desired, and close bag again. Toss until each piece is coated.

Brian, Amie and Jim Bosker are joined by their four-legged buddy Stewart for a weekend of camping, tailgating and a few good races! Brian says the group, from Columbus, Ohio, head to many different races during the season. "We always love to camp, and Stewart loves meeting new friends!"

Sam's Cheese Ball

According to Sam, he served this at a couple of football parties at Crawdaddy's and it was a big success. "It is better if made the day before."

3 (2½-ounce) packages thin beef, divided, chopped
3 (8-ounce) packages cream cheese, softened
1 tablespoon Ac'cent
1 tablespoon Worcestershire
1 or 2 bunches green scallions, chopped

Set aside 6–8 slices of beef. Chop rest of beef, and mix with remaining ingredients. Shape into a ball and cover with reserved chopped beef.

Submitted by Sam and Wes

Speedway Spread

1 (5-ounce) can boned chicken, drained
1 (8-ounce) package cream cheese, softened
3 tablespoons steak sauce
Dash of garlic powder
Dash of hot sauce
Salt and pepper to taste

Combine chicken with cream cheese, then combine with the remaining ingredients. Chill and serve with crackers, or make mini sandwiches for the race.

Submitted by Linda K. – North Carolina – Kasey Kahne fan

HEY RACE FANS, did you know that BACE Motorsports was started by Bill Baumgardner, founder of StaffAmerica? The team name BACE comes from the names of his children: Brian, Anna, Carrie and Emily.

DIPS AND SALSAS

Ray's Beer Dip

A nice dip. Made from . . . yes, some beer!

1 package ranch dip mix
2 (8-ounce) bars cream cheese, softened
½ (12-ounce) can cold beer
½ cup shredded pepper cheese

Mix everything together and chill. Great with crackers and pretzels.

Submitted by Ray and his crew – Talladega and Daytona race fans

Cheese Soup Dip

2 (10¾-ounce) cans Cheddar cheese soup
1 (10-ounce) can hot Ro-Tel
½ cup finely chopped pepperoni

Mix in a saucepan, and simmer on low about 15 minutes. Don't boil; just cook long enough to get the pepperoni heated up so the juices will spread.

Submitted by Cal L. – Darlington / Martinsville camper

Mushroom Soup Dip

1 (10¾-ounce) can cream of mushroom soup
½ cup melted processed cheese
½ cup bacon bits

In a saucepan, mix everything together and cook over low heat until smooth. Serve warm.

Submitted by Mary Beth N. – Race camper

Nix Racing Tires

Marilyn, Greg and Jennifer Nix
205-647-5570

Every race, the Nix family brings their business to the track. "We supply tires to the drivers and teams." According to Marilyn, her husband started the business in the mid-70s and they have made so many friends along the way that there is no way to count them. "We know so many great people. Racing people are great people," Marilyn said with a huge smile.

According to Marilyn, the business is a family affair, but her daughter Jennifer also has other talents. "She is a skilled surgery tech. She works on a transplant team." But racing is still in the blood. During this race weekend a birthday party was taking place for Jennifer's daughter Analeigh. "It's her first birthday!" All around, the Nix Racing Tires customers, friends, family, drivers and teams were enjoying cake, fruit and nuts in honor of the birthday.

As Jennifer cut cake for everyone, Marilyn told me they travel several tracks and follow the SAS tour in stocks and trucks. "We cover the Southeast. When we do get time to cook, I prefer country-style cooking while Greg loves to grill." Just then Jennifer brought me a HUGE slice of cake, fresh cherries and more. "You have to try the cake! It's my baby's birthday!" she said with a smile.

Cool and Spicy Dip

1 cup sour cream
½ cup hot sauce
2 tablespoons chili powder
1 teaspoon garlic powder
¼ cup finely minced onion
1 (4-ounce) can diced green chiles

Mix all, place in covered container, and chill before serving.

Sam's Vegetable Dip

1 cup mayonnaise
⅔ cup wine vinegar
½ teaspoon salt
⅛ teaspoon thyme
½ teaspoon curry powder
2 teaspoons chili sauce
2 teaspoons chopped chives (optional)
2 teaspoons grated onions
Dill weed and garlic salt to taste

Mix well and chill. This is excellent with raw veggies.

Submitted by Sam and Wes

Ham and French Onion Dip

1 (16-ounce) container sour cream
½ cup finely chopped sandwich ham
1 package onion soup mix
½ cup finely chopped corn beef
1 tablespoon paprika

Mix all together and chill serve cold with crackers and veggies.

Submitted by Carol J. – SAS Series crew member

Creamy Artichoke Dip

Megan, from Dover International Speedway, says that this recipe is perfect for not only tailgates, but parties as well. Hope you enjoy it!

2 (8-ounce) packages cream cheese, softened
⅓ cup sour cream
¼ cup mayonnaise
1 tablespoon fresh lemon juice
1 tablespoon Dijon mustard
1 garlic clove, minced
1 teaspoon Worcestershire sauce
½ teaspoon hot pepper sauce
3 (6-ounce) jars marinated artichoke hearts, drained, coarsely chopped
1 cup grated mozzarella cheese
3 green onions, finely chopped
2 teaspoons minced, seeded jalapeño

Using electric mixer, beat first 8 ingredients in large bowl to blend. Fold in artichokes, mozzarella cheese, green onions and jalapeño. Transfer to a 11x7x2-inch glass baking dish. (Can be made ahead; cover and refrigerate until ready to cook.) Bake at 400° until bubbling and brown on top, about 20 minutes. Serve warm with bread, crackers or pita.

Submitted by Megan L. Gill – Dover International Speedway

Deck Chef Tip!

Keep your cool

Vegetable dip recipes are real crowd pleasers. They taste great, and they're an excellent way to get people to eat their veggies. Before serving the vegetables, cut them up and put them in ice water for an hour to make them cool and crisp. Also, put the dip bowl in a bowl of ice when left out, in order to keep it cold.

Barney's Spinach Dip

Barney is a true sports fan. He can watch hours of sports on the TV and then just take a quick nap at a moment's notice while curled up on the couch.

1 package Knorr's Vegetable soup mix
1 (8-ounce) can water chestnuts, finely chopped
1 (8-ounce) package sour cream
2 (10-ounce) packages frozen spinach

Combine all of the ingredients except the spinach. Thaw and drain spinach as much as possible. Chop into very small pieces. Combine with the dip mix, chill and serve.

Submitted by Barney Nagem – Kerry Earnhart / War Eagle fan

Spinach Dip

1 package chopped spinach, drained
1 cup sour cream
1 cup mayonnaise
¼ cup Parmesan cheese
1 package favorite dip mix
1 (8-ounce) can sliced water chestnuts

Make sure the spinach is drained well. Dry with paper towels. Combine with remaining ingredients except water chestnuts. Drain the water chestnuts and dice into small pieces. Add to dip. Cover and chill before serving.

Submitted by John L. – Dad of go-kart driver

HEY RACE FANS, did you know that when NEXTEL became the new series sponsor in 2003, it ended the Winston association with NASCAR which had lasted for 33 years?

Jim's Crab Dip

"A good crab dip is a must in my house." According to Jim, this dip is a must at all of his race-day events.

2 (7½-ounce) cans white crabmeat, drained
2 (8-ounce) packages cream cheese, softened
½ cup chopped onion
1 tablespoon minced garlic
1 tablespoon milk
1 tablespoon horseradish

Mix all together and place in a small oven-safe dish. Bake at 350° for 15–20 minutes. Serve hot.

Submitted by Jim S. – Jimmy Spencer fan

Jake Says—

Make some mini shrimp poppers. Just take some corn bread mix and add minced shrimp. Toss in some spices and cook them like you do hushpuppies.

Hot Crab Dip

1 (8-ounce) package cream cheese, softened
1 cup mayo
2 teaspoons lemon juice
1 teaspoon Worcestershire
½ teaspoon Old Bay Seasoning
1 pound fresh crabmeat, drained well

Add cream cheese and mayo to a small slow cooker; mix until well blended. Add remaining ingredients; mix until well blended. Cook on LOW heat. Serve with crackers or warm bread.

Submitted by Karen Ptak – Dover International Speedway

Sue's Michigan International Speedway Shrimp Dip

2 (4-ounce) cans tiny shrimp, drained
1 (16-ounce) container sour cream
¼ cup finely chopped green onions
2 tablespoons ketchup
1 tablespoon prepared horseradish

Chop shrimp, if desired. Mix all ingredients until well blended. Cover and refrigerate several hours or until well chilled.

Submitted by Sue Malewitz – MIS Cookbook
Used with permission of Michigan International Speedway

Cream Cheese Pineapple Dip

1 (8-ounce) package cream cheese, softened
⅔ cup finely grated mild Cheddar cheese
1 (8-ounce) container sour cream
1 (8-ounce) can crushed pineapple, drained

Combine all ingredients and chill before serving. This dip is thick. You can add a bit more sour cream to make it thinner, or more cream cheese to make a cheese ball. Serve with fruit.

Steve's Canned Chili Dip

A quick dip that is almost too easy to make. Of course that's what makes tailgating fun—coming up with something that seems hard, but is so easy it knocks people's socks off!

2 (16-ounce) cans chili
1 (16-ounce) jar cheese dip
1 (8-ounce) bar cream cheese
Hot sauce (optional)

Combine everything in a nonstick pan, and heat until cream cheese is melted. "I like to add hot sauce, and I NEVER use that cheap hot dog chili mushy stuff."

Submitted by Steve and Lori

Gerald's Texas Caviar

Even though Gerald is not from Texas, he is a Texas fan. "I went to my first race in Texas while I was there on business. I have been a race fan ever since. I've been to Cup races, ARCA and ASA, and I love hitting local dirt tracks when I'm in a small town." Here is Gerald's race-day Texas Caviar recipe. "It works good at the races, in my den watching the race and even on Super Bowl Sunday!"

1 can pinto beans
1 can black-eyed peas
1 can white corn
1 small jar pimento, chopped
1 small jar jalapeño peppers, chopped
1 (4-ounce) can green chiles
1 onion, chopped
½ cup cider vinegar
⅓ cup oil
⅓ cup sugar
1 tablespoon salt
1 tablespoon pepper
½ tablespoon garlic powder
Hot sauce to taste

Drain all of the canned items. Mix beans, peas, corn, pimento, jalapeños, chiles and onion in a bowl, and stir. Combine everything else in a pot and boil about 5 minutes to melt sugar. Pour over the bean mix, cover and chill. According to Gerald, it's best to allow the caviar to stand about an hour.

Submitted by Gerald W., Jr. – Lexington, KY – Mark Martin fan

Michael Ritch

Driver – NASCAR Craftsman Truck
NASCAR Weekly – USAR Hooters Pro Cup
#28 Jackaroo Sauces Dodge

When you want to talk racing and cooking with some stock car guys, you have to touch base with Michael Ritch. When I asked Michael what he would cook or want served for his family and friends during a big Daytona 500 get-together, he quickly responded, "I love ribs cooked on a grill or smoker and covered in Jackaroo Sauce." That's a great answer considering Michael drives the #28 Jackaroo Sauce car in the USAR Pro Cup. But you could tell by talking to Michael that he loves talking about racing, his sponsors and his family. "This is my son. We call him Big Jake!"

Michael started like many drivers in North Carolina. "I started at about age seven racing BMX, carts and such around High Point. I moved into racing because somebody stole my old yard cart and I asked Santa for a go-kart with a motor. Well, my dad told me he talked to Santa who said if I got a go-kart, it would have to be used for racing. I said OK!"

According to Michael, his dad taught him all about racing and owning a team. "He did it all, and he taught me." I asked Michael about the racing life passing onto his young son Jacob Austin. "Hopefully he'll take up golf!" Michael said with a smile.

ACHIEVEMENTS: North Carolina Dirt Champion, Horseman Gold Cup Champion, 10 wins in stock series, 26 top-five finishes, 43 top-ten finishes

Bristol Bean Dip and Homemade Corn Chips

A friend of mine who loves NASCAR (and racing in general) gave me this recipe for her bean dip. It is a great recipe. But if you don't have time to make some really easy chips, just buy a bag.

2 (16-ounce) cans fat-free refried beans (HAR!)
1 (4.5-ounce) can chopped chiles
1 tablespoon steak sauce
½ cup shredded Jack cheese
¼ cup minced onion
1 tablespoon cumin powder
1 tablespoon hot sauce
1 package small corn tortillas
Chili powder
Cajun seasoning

Combine all ingredients except tortillas, chili powder and Cajun seasoning. Heat slowly in a bowl in the microwave. Using a pizza cutter, cut each tortilla into 4 equal pizza-style slices. Fry in oil or bake in an oven until crisp. As soon as you remove the tortilla chips from the oil, sprinkle lightly with chili powder and Cajun seasoning.

PHOTO BY KC RACING GRAPHICS

Fans, cars, trucks and more are all packed into Bristol Motor Speedway before the start of a night of racing.

Easy Bean Dip

2 (16-ounce) cans refried beans
1 (4-ounce) can green chiles
1 small onion, minced
½ cup shredded cheese
1 tablespoon cumin powder
1 tablespoon garlic powder
1 tablespoon chili powder
1 tablespoon Worcestershire
1 tablespoon hot sauce

Combine everything and mix well. Bake in an oven about 30 minutes at 300°. Serve hot with chips and sour cream.

Submitted by R. S. – Daytona tailgater and fan

Lori's Tex-Mex Pork and Bean Dip

This is a neat recipe for bean dip, which is, in reality, a great recipe for baked beans! Just make the recipe, toss it in a blender or food processor, cook and serve with chips. Very tasty!

2 (16-ounce) cans baked beans
½ cup minced onion
½ cup brown sugar
½ tablespoon grape jelly
⅔ cup shredded Jack cheese

Combine all ingredients except cheese. Blend with a fork or toss in the blender about 10 seconds. Place in an oven-safe dish, and bake at 350° about 30 minutes. Top with cheese before serving.

Submitted by Steve and Lori

Tex-Mex Dip

1 (16-ounce) can refried beans
1 package taco seasoning
1 (8-ounce) bar cream cheese, softened
1 (16-ounce) can chili with meat
1 cup grated cheese

Mix the refried beans and taco seasoning together. In a microwave-safe dish, layer the beans, then the cream cheese, then the chili and top with grated cheese. Microwave until cheese is melted.

Submitted by James P., Jr. – NASCAR camper and tailgate fan

Brad's HOT Velveeta Dip

Brad says he makes this for camping at the track or just watching the race at home. "It used to be a ton hotter but my wife thought I made it that hot just to bug people, so I took out some of the peppers and stuff." It's still plenty hot!

1 (1-pound) block Velveeta cheese
1 (16-ounce) jar hot salsa
1 pound hot sausage
¼ cup hot sauce
½ cup milk

Combine everything in a saucepan or crockpot, and cook over low heat until melted and smooth.

Submitted by Brad and his crew – Bristol campers

Taco Salad Dip

1 package taco seasoning mix
2 (8-ounce) packages cream cheese, softened
1 (16-ounce) carton sour cream
1 package shredded lettuce
1 tomato, chopped
1 (4-ounce) can chopped black olives
1 package shredded Mexican cheese
1 package tortilla chips

Blend together in large bowl, taco seasoning mix, cream cheese and sour cream. Spread the mixture on serving plate or dish. Top with chopped lettuce, tomato, olives and shredded cheese. Garnish sides of dish with tortilla chips and serve.

Submitted by Donna Robbins

HEY RACE FANS, did you know that roof flaps were first used in NASCAR in 1994? This simple safety feature was designed to keep a car from becoming airborne during a spin, or if the car were to turn backwards.

Cheeseburger Dip

A great dip for your favorite corn or tortilla chips—thick and hearty with tons of flavor!

1 pound ground beef, browned
1 small onion, diced
1 (8-ounce) can tomato sauce
1 (8-ounce) package cream cheese
½ cup grated Parmesan cheese
¼ cup shredded Cheddar cheese
1 tablespoon minced garlic
1 teaspoon oregano
1 teaspoon cumin powder
1 tablespoon parsley
1 tablespoon sugar

Brown ground beef with onions; drain. Add remaining ingredients, and stir over low heat until cheese melts. Serve hot.

Karen's Speedway Salsa Dip

Karen of North Carolina says she is the biggest Dale Jarrett fan ever. "I love those commercials!" When Karen sets up her tailgates in RV land, she always has plenty of extra snacks. "You meet so many people, you have to have some extra food for your new friends."

½ pound ground beef, browned, drained
1 (2-pound) package Velveeta cheese, melted
1 package taco seasoning
1 (10-ounce) can diced tomatoes and chiles
2 tablespoons hot sauce
Garlic powder to taste

Just mix it all up and serve warm with some chips and crackers. "I sometimes add a squirt or two of lime juice for some extra flavor," says Karen.

Submitted by Karen – North Carolina – Dale Jarrett fan

Patti Gross

Mark Gibson Racing ARCA
www.markgibson.com

When I was visiting an ARCA race and chatting with teams and drivers, a name came up several times. "You have to meet Patti!" I was told this several times over. Everyone said Patti cooked some of the best home-cooked meals that I would ever taste. Well, they were right! Patti cooks about 95% of the Mark Gibson racing team's meals for a race weekend while still in the comfort of her own kitchen.

"I really don't have a secret. I just cook it at home then vacuum-seal the meals." Yep, it's that easy. Patti whips up some traditional home-cooked meals that any grandmother would be proud of, seals the food and then heats it up at the track.

According to Patti, the method not only provides great food, but also provides a few bonus features as well. "Since I really only have to boil water to heat the vacuum bags, I can concentrate on other team needs. Plus, if we plan on lunch at 12 noon and something goes wrong, a ton of food is not wasted. Prep time is nothing and there is little waste."

Patti says no meal is beyond her vac-pack method. "Everyone loves French toast. I can freeze up to 12 slices of HUGE French toast pieces per package. Then just heat up and serve!"

PATTI GROSS' TAILGATE TIP: Marinate meats using your marinade and a vac sealer. The vac method will actually suck the marinade right into the meat."

Best Guacamole EVER

That's what Terry told me! Terry and his crew visit up to five races a year. "Atlanta, Bristol, Lowes, Nashville and of course, Talledega BABY!" Here is Terry's guacamole dip. "This is the Best Guacamole EVER! You'll never buy store-bought again!"

4 ripe avocados
1 small tomato
1 small onion
1 tablespoon lime juice
2 tablespoons mayonnaise
Salt and pepper to taste

Peel and pit the avocados, and mash with a fork. Peel and dice the tomato into small pieces; pat dry with paper towels. Combine all ingredients and mix well. Store in an airtight container with as little air as possible to prevent the color from changing. Serve chilled with chips.

Submitted by Terry – Jeffereson, GA – Kenny Wallace fan

Simple Salsa

1 (16-ounce) jar picante sauce
1 medium onion, chopped
1 green pepper, chopped
1 (14½-ounce) can diced tomatoes, drained
1 teaspoon cumin powder
Salt, pepper and garlic powder to taste

Mix everything together in a bowl; cover and place in the fridge for a few hours before serving.

Submitted by Erica W.

Kris's Bean Salsa

2 tablespoons chopped cilantro
1 large onion, finely chopped
2 (4-ounce) cans green chiles
1 (16-ounce) can black beans, drained
1 (14½-ounce) can diced tomatoes, drained
1 tablespoon cumin powder
1 tablespoon lemon juice

Combine all ingredients and chill.

Submitted by Kris McCloud – Dirt track fan

Hot Pepper Salsa

This recipe comes from Martin and Becky. I met them at a fan day in Atlanta for a Hooters Pro Cup race. They were on the way to the mountains and had pulled off the interstate when they noticed the race cars and haulers outside of the Kroger supermarket. Becky commented, "We love racing. We just needed some groceries for camping, and saw this. What a treat." After meeting some drivers and getting a few autographs, Becky was kind enough to give me her "super semi-secret" salsa recipe.

2 (14½-ounce) cans diced tomatoes, drained
1 medium red onion, chopped
1 medium white onion, chopped
1 medium red bell pepper, chopped
2–3 jalapeño peppers, minced
2 tablespoons chopped cilantro
½ tablespoon garlic powder
1 tablespoon red wine vinegar
1 tablespoon olive oil
Large dash of cumin powder

"I mix all of this up about two or three days before the race—either when we camp, or just for the races we watch on TV. If you let it sit covered in the fridge for a day or two, it tastes so much better."

Submitted by Martin and Becky H. – Kyle Petty fans

Cheaters Salsa

Randy and Katie say they have mastered the art of opening jars and cans and making regular store-bought foods better. Here is their easy recipe for salsa that feeds a bunch.

1 (16-ounce) jar salsa
4 small packets taco sauce
1 (16-ounce) can whole-kernel corn
1 (16-ounce) can black beans, drained
1 tablespoon lemon or lime juice

Mix well, then chill before serving.

Submitted by Randy and Katie G. – North Carolina – Race fans

GREEN FLAG RACING

It's time for some green flag racing! Main dishes are what it's all about. At any speedway on any race weekend, you can find the best in cooking. From turkey legs to ribs, main courses are on grills and smokers across the campgrounds. When I went to my first big NASCAR race in college, I was amazed at the effort people put into their food. Burgers, dogs and chicken were, of course, everywhere. There was also an abundance of cold cuts and snacks. Today, the art of speedway cooking has advanced almost as much as the cars themselves! With today's modern HUGE gas and charcoal tow-behind grills and RV's, complete kitchens have come to the tracks. Did I mention crockpots, griddles, smokers and more? Here is a collection of recipes for all of your basic main dish items. These recipes can be made at home or at your next tailgate. Now let's get to some green flag cooking!

- Beef and Burgers
- Pork
- Chicken and Turkey
- Seafood
- Sauces, Rubs and Marinades

BEEF & BURGERS

Oven-Style Beef Ribs

These ribs are made before the big event and the final touch is done at the tailgate over some flames and some smoke. A great rib dish that is stacked with flavor and easy to prepare.

3 pounds beef short ribs
2 bottles beer
Soul seasoning, or your favorite rub
1 (20-ounce) can pineapple chunks
1 (18-ounce) bottle favorite barbecue sauce

In a baking dish or pan, place the ribs and pour in the beer. Cover with a generous amount of the seasoning. Cover and chill overnight or for as long as possible.

Cook, lightly covered, in a 350° oven for about 1 hour. Check for tenderness, add more seasoning and rotate the ribs, if needed. When done, remove from oven and allow to cool before placing in a zip-close bag. At the track, open pineapples and mash with a fork. Combine with barbecue sauce. Baste ribs and reheat slowly on the grill over low to medium heat.

Note: This recipe is just as delicious using country-style pork ribs.

Beef Ribs

2 pounds beef short ribs
1 beer
1 (8-ounce) can crushed pineapple
1 (8-ounce) jar pepper jelly
1 (18-ounce) bottle favorite barbecue sauce

Marinate ribs in beer, pineapple with juice and pepper jelly. Cook on grill as slowly as possible, basting occasionally with barbecue sauce and leftover marinade.

Submitted by Carol L. – Atlanta, GA – Jefferson Speedway

BBQ Grilled Beef Ribs

When you hit the campgrounds around the stock car world, get ready to eat some good ribs!

4–5 pounds beef ribs
½ cup apple cider vinegar
½ cup soy sauce
2 tablespoons garlic powder
1 tablespoon chili powder
Barbecue sauce

Place ribs in a large dish or pan, or cut up and put into zip-close bags. Soak as long as possible in a mixture of vinegar, soy sauce, garlic powder and chili powder. Grill over low to medium heat until done. Baste with remaining juice as needed. Before removing from grill, coat with barbecue sauce. Serve hot.

Submitted by Richard – NASCAR / BUSCH / ARCA / ASA fan

Peter Gibbons

Driver – BUSCH, NASCAR, CASCAR
www.petergibbons.com

Besides traveling and a good auction, Peter Gibbons loves racing. This Canadian-born driver became interested in the sport at an early age and began racing at regional tracks in Canada and the northern U.S.

Peter has raced in the BUSCH Grand National Series, the NASCAR Cup Series, and regional series, but now makes his home in CASCAR.

According to wife Denise, it has been an around-the-world trip for a sponsor. "It's kind of strange. We moved the whole family and shop to North Carolina to seek a sponsor for our BUSCH and NASCAR efforts. We even set up a business. Next thing you know, we landed a National Sponsor for the CASCAR Series."

"It's made for some hectic travel." But Denise says it has been worth it. "Our sponsors are great. The team is very understanding with the crazy travel schedule, but things have fallen into place."

Peter drove his #1 Canadian Tire Monte Carlo into a second-place finish in points during the 2004 season—so they must be doing something right.

NEAT THING: Peter is a huge Harley Davidson fan.

Racing Ribs

4 racks ribs
1 quart honey
½ gallon soy sauce
1 quart favorite barbecue sauce

Cut racks down to 2-rib sections. Put in large pot with water. Add honey and soy sauce. Boil till ribs are thoroughly cooked, then remove from heat. Keep them in the broth, and marinate 2–4 hours in the refrigerator.

Grill ribs over low heat 5 minutes, then baste with barbecue sauce, and grill 10 minutes longer. Enjoy!

Submitted by Steve Herbert – Forked River, NJ
Gasman for Norm Bennings, ARCA #84

Southwestern-Style Prime Rib Roast

3 tablespoons chili powder
2 tablespoons cumin powder
2 tablespoons paprika
1 tablespoon salt
1 tablespoon pepper
1 tablespoon garlic powder
1 prime rib beef roast

Make a rub out of the dry ingredients and rub firmly into the prime rib. Cover with cling wrap and place in the fridge overnight or for as long as possible.

Use indirect heat and grill fat-side-up. Allow to rest, covered with foil, on the coolest part of the grill about 10 minutes before slicing.

Submitted by Parker – Texas Motor Speedway fan

Speedway Pot Roast

A quick idea for a pot roast—this recipe was actually cooked at home and brought to the track after being frozen and vac-packed.

1 beef roast
1 cup water
1 package beef stew seasoning
Diced potatoes
Diced onions
Diced carrots

Place the roast on the grill, and sear outside over high heat till brown. Place the roast in a large foil pan with water. Rub with the beef stew seasoning. Add veggies and cover with foil. Cook in oven or on covered grill until done. Depending on how thick your roast is, cooking time can be about 20–25 minutes per pound.

Jarred's Beef Roast

This recipe is from Jarred who says it works great with beef or pork. "I cook it over my grill using a spit. I also use a drip pan so I can baste it with its own juices."

1 (6-pound) beef roast
Minced garlic
Salt and pepper to taste
Olive oil
Steak sauce
Worcestershire sauce

Make several long slits along the outside of the roast, and rub with garlic, salt and pepper. Baste with olive oil, steak sauce amd Worcestershire. Cook, using a spit; baste often. Cook over medium heat.

Submitted by Jarred N. – Kansas

HEY RACE FANS, did you know that 1990 Daytona 500 winner, broadcaster, NEXTEL and BUSCH Series driver Derrike Cope is an accomplished baseball player? His position was catcher and he was scouted by pro scouts before an injury ended his baseball career and turned him to racing full time.

Easy Barbecue Shank Steaks

4 cheap shank steaks
½ cup barbecue dry rub
1 cup barbecue sauce
Sliced onions
Cheese

Before the tailgate, rub the steaks with the barbecue rub and seal in a covered dish or zip-close bag. Brush with your favorite barbecue sauce as you grill. When the steaks are just about done, put some onions and cheese in the center, and fold like you would an omelette.

Submitted by J. T. – Petty "The King" fan

Excitement builds as the fans and drivers get ready for green flag racing.

Easy Italian Steaks with Cheese Sauce

Richard says he stole this recipe from a guy camping next to him at a race a few years back. "It's his. I give credit where credit is due." Richard says this is so easy, it makes him look good!

4 steaks of your choice
1 bottle Italian dressing
¼ cup milk
1 cup Velveeta cheese cubes
Bit of butter
Garlic powder to taste
Parsley

Marinate the steaks in the Italian dressing as long as possible, then grill as desired. While grilling, put the milk and Velveeta in a saucepan, and melt the cheese. Add a bit of butter, garlic powder and parsley. Stir until smooth. Drizzle over steaks before serving.

Submitted by Richard – NASCAR / BUSCH / ARCA / ASA fan

Deck Chef Tip!

Often less is more.

A traditionally seasoned steak cooked medium-well offers great flavor. (Traditionally means using butter as a baste with a simple salt-and-pepper rub.)

Always let your steak rest off of the grill for a few minutes before serving. This rest period allows the steak to continue to cook in its own juices for a few minutes. This allows for a more tender steak. But a steak cooked well-done will not have as much juice as a medium-well steak because more fat has been cooked off.

Honey Mustard Steaks

I really whittled down the ingredients in this recipe to let more of the steak flavor come through, and still have the fun taste of the honey mustard. You could use beef, pork, venison, chicken or whatever you enjoy.

6 boneless steaks of your choice
½ cup Dijon mustard
¼ cup honey
1 teaspoon salt
1 teaspoon pepper

Bring your steaks to room temperature, and brush with all of the combined ingredients. Grill as you like. Serve hot with French bread.

Sesame Grilled Steak

½ cup soy sauce
⅓ cup grape juice
½ cup sesame oil
1 small onion, diced
3 tablespoons brown sugar
1 tablespoon ground ginger
Salt and pepper to taste
Steaks of your choice
Sesame seeds, toasted

Mix everything together except the steak and sesame seeds. Marinate steaks of your choice as long as possible. Grill until done, then top with toasted sesame seeds.

Salt and Pepper Steaks

4 rib-eye steaks
Olive oil
2 tablespoons salt
2 tablespoons pepper

Marinate the steaks in olive oil about an hour. Rub the salt and pepper into the steaks, and wrap as tightly as possible with cling wrap. Chill for several hours. Grill over medium-high heat. Turn as little as possible. Baste with more olive oil (or melted butter).

Submitted by J. T. – Petty "The King" fan

Big Show Food's - Cadbury's Ye Olde London Broil

My buddy Big Tom Price markets John Boy and Billy food items. One way he does this is to visit racetracks, set up "Grillzilla" and feed hungry John Boy and Billy race fans. "I meet great people every day!"

1½ pounds flank steak
1 cup John Boy and Billy's Grillin' Sauce
2 tablespoons Worcestershire sauce
1 tablespoon prepared English mustard
½ teaspoon garlic powder

Lay the flank steak out and, with a fork, pierce each side 50–60 times. Combine John Boy and Billy's Grillin' Sauce, Worcestershire sauce, mustard and garlic powder. Brush the flank steak with sauce. Grill or broil until desired degree of doneness, basting with the sauce every minute or so. When done, slice the London Broil thinly and on the diagonal, against the grain. John Boy likes it with Garlic Mashed Potatoes and Grilled Vegetables.

Used with permission of Big Tom Price
www.bigshowfoods.com

HEY RACE FANS, did you know that John Isley and Billy James are John Boy and Billy, creators of The Big Show, a radio powerhouse originating in Charlotte, North Carolina, and syndicated in 111 markets across 23 states? The Big Show audience numbers approximately two million households in any average quarter hour, and it has been estimated that twenty million people listen every morning—approximately 15% of the entire listening radio audience across the U.S.

Big Tom Price

Big Show Foods
Home of John Boy and Billy's Grillin' Sauce
www.bigshowfoods.com

I know Big Tom was featured in my first cookbook about Appalachian barbecue, BUT he has to be in this book as well. Big Tom Price is the town crier when it comes to John Boy and Billy's Grillin' Sauce and www.bigshowfoods.com.

Big Tom loves his job marketing John Boy and Billy sauces and food products so much that he has turned it into an exact science. "What better place to show off award-winning sauces and recipes than the ultimate tailgate party . . . racetracks and barbecue cook-offs?" Big Tom and his buddies, Fred and Carl and the crew, pull the John Boy and Billy Grillzilla around the stock car circuit feeding hungry fans and teams the best in grilled foods. Then they hit the barbecue cook-off circuit.

When a race weekend is not on the schedule, they head off to win a few trophies and medals in barbecue cook-offs. "Racing and cooking is a great way to say thanks to John Boy and Billy fans. It's also a great way to promote www.bigshowfoods.com and John Boy and Billy's Grillin' Sauce."

Keep an eye out, you may catch a car running around a track with the John Boy and Billy's Grillin' Sauce logo on the hood or on the side of a smoker near you.

Texas-Style Grilled Flat Fajita

Are you looking for a great recipe for some cheap steak? Here is one you can grill at the track or on the back porch for your race-day party!

1 tablespoon paprika
2 teaspoons black pepper
1 tablespoon hot sauce
1 teaspoon sugar
1 teaspoon chopped cilantro
1 teaspoon cumin powder
2 pounds shank steak
1 large green pepper, sliced
1 large red pepper, sliced
4 large onions, sliced
1 (12-ounce) can beer
1 lemon
Large tortillas
Grated cheese
Sour cream (optional)
Salsa (optional)

Combine the paprika, pepper, hot sauce, sugar, cilantro and cumin powder, and rub onto the steak. Wrap in cling wrap, and chill until you get to the grill at the track. Slice the veggies and set up your grill for direct medium-high heat. Grill the steak and veggies. Baste the steak with some beer; squirt with some lemon juice. When the steak is done, remove from heat and slice into thin strips. Place steak slices and veggies on a tortilla, top with some cheese and fold over. Place back on the grill to melt the cheese and warm the tortilla. Serve hot with some sour cream and salsa, if desired.

HEY RACE FANS, did you know the first Daytona 500 was not finished for three days? Officials took that time to study a photograph of the finish before they determined a winner!

Ultimate Tailgate Beef Kabobs

1 pound stew-cut steak
Steak sauce
Hot sauce
1 (20-ounce) can pineapple chunks
1 large onion, chopped large
1 bell pepper, chopped large
Steak-cut French fries, partially thawed

Marinate the steak cubes in the steak sauce, hot sauce and juice from the pineapples as long as possible. Place the steak and remaining ingredients on skewers. Make sure the French fries are still pretty solid. They cook faster than regular potatoes. But if they are too thawed, they will crumble and fall off the skewer. Brush with extra marinade while cooking over high heat.

Submitted by Derek P.

Steak Kabobs

Get you some thin-sliced steak. And I mean nothing but steak!

Flank or skirt steak, cut into strips
½ cup soy sauce
½ cup steak sauce
Cooked rice (optional)
Hot dog buns (optional)
Grilled onions (optional)
Shredded white American cheese

Beat the steak as thin as possible. Cut into long strips about the width of a piece of bacon. Marinate in the combination of soy and steak sauce. Place it on a skewer almost like a ribbon. Cook on the grill and serve with some rice. Or better yet, place the kabob—stick, steak and all—on a hot dog bun. Pull the stick out and top with some grilled onions and a bit of cheese for a great hot sandwich.

Tangy Beef on a Stick

Any meal served on a stick is bound to be fun! I love this recipe. It's easy, quick, full of flavor and sure to make your tailgating area smell great! Toss some of these on the grill and enjoy. This recipe comes from the dirt tracks of East Tennessee.

2 pounds shank steak
1 bottle teriyaki sauce
Ground ginger
Soy sauce

Cut the steak into thin strips and pound until very thin. Soak with teriyaki sauce, ginger and soy sauce for as long as possible. Thread onto kabob sticks and cook over medium heat until done.

Submitted by Jarred N. – Kansas – Dirt track fan

Beef and Cheesy Mac

Why buy a box of a hamburger meal, when you can make it yourself! Tony says you can add as much stuff to this dish as you like to spice it up. "I like the heat but others just like the regular flavor. I always add a few extras when I am making my bowl!"

1 pound ground beef
½ cup water
1 package stew mix
2 boxes mac and cheese
1 small onion, chopped
1 tablespoon minced garlic

Brown the ground beef, then drain. Mix in water and stew mix. Prepare the mac and cheese as per the directions. Mix in meat mix, onion and garlic. Toss in some hot peppers, hot sauce and such for more flavor. Serve hot.

Submitted by Tony R.

Pita Taco Burgers

1 pound ground beef
1 package taco seasoning
1 egg, beaten
½ cup cracker crumbs
3 pita bread shells, cut in half
Lettuce
Cheese
Onions

Combine ground beef and taco seasoning, egg and cracker crumbs. Form into 6 wide, thin patties. Cook until done, and place with your favorite toppings inside pita pockets.

Carol's Cup of Soup Burgers

2 pounds ground beef
1 package onion soup mix
1 egg, beaten
⅓ cup steak sauce

Mix up everything, shape into burgers and grill until done.

Submitted by Carol L. – Atlanta, GA – Jefferson Speedway

Deck Chef Tip!

Beef it up!

Sorry, leaner ground beef means less juicy burgers. You can add to the moisture content of your burgers by adding sauces to the meat before you make your patties. Too much sauce, such as barbecue sauce, may make the patties harder to form and stick together. So don't add too much!

Ultimate Burgers

It took me about an hour of conversation before this "super secret" Ultimate Burger recipe was given to me. According to Lisa, this recipe is a "sure thing, baby" come race day. Lisa is from the Atlanta area, and says, "Nothing beats a day at the races, except when Bulldog football is on!"

1 pound ground beef
1 package ranch dressing mix
4 packets Taco Bell Hot Sauce
1 egg, beaten

Combine all of the ingredients. Mix well, and form into 4–6 patties; grill until done. Of course, top with your favorite cheeses and trimmings.

Submitted by Lisa Hanning – Atlanta Motor Speedway / UGA fan

I love the Back Yard Burgers car. What self-respecting, race fan grill master wouldn't love a car like this?!

Buffalo Burgers

I have a friend who spends a lot of time around the dirt tracks. He suggested one day that somebody should find a way to make hamburgers taste like hot wings. Well, besides one being from a chicken and the other being from a cow . . . somehow this made sense. Of course we had been standing in the sun all day. But here is a neat twist on a simple burger.

1 stick butter
1 (5-ounce) bottle hot sauce
2 pounds ground beef

In a saucepan or skillet, melt the butter, add the hot sauce and stir. Allow to cool but not harden. Add the ground beef and mix well. Form patties, grill, and serve topped with pepper cheese.

Note: The butter and the sauce is an original hot wing recipe.

Cheese Burgers

A very simple recipe from a very nice tailgating fan.

1 pound ground beef
½ cup finely shredded Cheddar cheese
2 tablespoons Parmesan cheese
Salt and pepper to taste
Onion powder

Combine everything and shape into burgers. Cook until done. Top with all of your burger fixings!

Submitted by the Tucker family – NASCAR tailgate fans

HEY RACE FANS, did you know that Randy LaJoie was the first NASCAR Busch Series driver to win over $1 million in a single race season (1997)?

Steve Radney and Skippy Hutton

Kyle Busch Team Lowe's Racing

I was in the media center at a NASCAR BUSCH race sending in a story when I met Kerry Gilbert, media contact for Kyle Busch driver #5 Lowe's Chevrolet Monte Carlo. When Kerry found out I was writing race stories and I was a cookbook author, his comment was simple, "I have two guys you have to meet!"

When Steve and Skippy are not driving the trucks or motor coaches for Kyle Busch, they can often be found around the motor coach kitchen or along their very impressive grill in the garage area. "Cooking for the crew is our second job!" Steve said with a smile. According to Skippy, real name never given, cooking is the fun part. "Sure, we do other things like act as the second gasman in the pits and such, but you should see our new grill!" Steve added that as long as he has been in racing, the team cook has been bred into the industry. "Its been that way since I have been in the sport, from Cup teams on down."

According to both of Team Lowe's garage chefs, the menu can vary from track to track. "Just kind of depends on the day, times, etc." Breakfast is a favorite among most teams and Steve and Skippy dish up a great first meal with "Signature Sausage Gravy." When I asked Skippy for his favorite grilling Super Bowl / Daytona race-day menu for friends and family, the answer was quick, "Gotta have chili and some great filets!"

Simple Cheesy Sloppy Joes

Simple and good, on a bun or just by the spoonful.

2 pounds ground beef
1 onion, chopped
1 cup shredded cheese
1 green bell pepper, minced
1 bottle favorite barbecue sauce
1 (10-ounce) can Ro-Tel
Hot sauce
Salt and pepper to taste

Brown meat and drain the fat. Mix everything together and simmer until thick. Serve on a bun, or eat in a bowl with a spoon!

Submitted by Ray and his crew – Talladega / Daytona race fans

Tailgate Sloppy Joes

Here is a quick and VERY easy recipe for some homemade sloppy joes. This recipe is courtesy of Barbara from North Carolina who says it's a favorite meal in her RV at just about any race or football game.

1 pound ground beef
½ pound ground pork or sausage
1 onion, finely diced
1 (8-ounce) can tomato sauce
1 cup water
½ cup sugar
¼ cup Worcestershire sauce
1 tablespoon minced garlic
1 teaspoon black pepper
1 teaspoon salt

Brown and drain beef and sausage. Break into small pieces with a spoon or fork. Combine with remaining ingredients in a skillet and cook until excess water cooks off. "I like to add some hot sauce or more salt and pepper if it needs it. I have even minced up some red peppers and added it as well," says Barbara.

Submitted by Barbara – North Carolina – Tony Stewart / UNC fan

Meat and Potatoes on the Grill

Easy to make and easy to serve.

6 baking potatoes, washed and sliced
1 pound ground beef
1 tablespoon minced garlic
Salt and pepper to taste
1 stick butter or margarine
6 slices raw bacon
1 onion, diced
2 tablespoons Cajun seasoning
Grated cheese, your choice

Make this in a large heavy-duty foil pan. Wash and slice potatoes to make ¼-inch-wide chips. Combine ground beef with garlic and salt and pepper. Make into small patties and place on the grill. Combine remaining ingredients except cheese in foil pan. Cover and cook on grill using medium high heat. Cook for about 30 minutes while burgers are cooking; check for burning. Remove burger patties from grill, and using a fork break into small pieces. Add meat and cheese to potatoes and mix well. Place back on grill and cook until cheese melts. Serve hot.

Bubba Stew

I tried a stew like this at a USAR Hooters Pro Cup race, or was it an SAS Southern All Stars Race . . . ? Heck, it doesn't matter. The point is, this is my version of what I was told was Bubba Stew. It was served in a bowl with a slice of corn bread and some cheese.

1 pound ground beef
½ small onion, minced
½ tablespoon minced garlic
¾ cup minced mushrooms
1 (8-ounce) can tomato sauce
1 tablespoon Worcestershire sauce
1 (16-ounce) can kidney beans, undrained
1 (16-ounce) can whole-kernel corn,
Salt and pepper to taste
Favorite cheese, grated

Brown ground beef, then drain. Add remaining ingredients, except cheese. Simmer until stew thickens. Serve hot topped with cheese.

Hamburger Pie

1 pound ground beef
1 onion, diced
1 (10 3/4-ounce) can tomato soup
1 (16-ounce) can mixed veggies, drained
1 package taco seasoning
Salt and pepper to taste
Jiffy Corn Bread Mix

Brown ground beef in a skillet, then drain. Add onion, tomato soup, veggies and taco seasoning; mix well. Salt and pepper to taste. Place into a baking dish. Make the corn bread mix according to directions on box, and spoon it on top. Bake until corn bread is golden brown.

Submitted by Derek P.

Jackie Ballard says his homemade, custom-built smoker/grill combo can be charcoal, wood or even gas fired. "I've taken this thing to Titans games, Talladega, Daytona, Bristol and more." The secret according to Jackie is making sure you get started early because you never know when people are going to get hungry. This smoker/grill combo can cook unlimited burgers and dogs, countless ribs and butts all to perfection. "I can regulate the heat good and make some great race-day barbecue on this. I can tow it anywhere!"

Grilled Meatloaf

½ cup ketchup
½ cup quick-cooking oats
¼ cup chopped green pepper
1 egg, beaten
1 teaspoon dried parsley flakes
1 teaspoon Worcestershire sauce
½ teaspoon garlic powder
½ teaspoon dried basil
¼ teaspoon pepper
2 pounds ground beef
Additional ketchup (optional)

In a large bowl, combine all ingredients except meat. Crumble beef over mixture and mix well. Shape into 2 loaves. Linda says, "I use the upper rack of the grill, so I make the shape kind of flat." Place a sheet of heavy-duty foil in center of grill. Place meat loaves on foil boat (do not seal foil). Grill with cover closed over indirect medium heat for 50 minutes (can be turned at 25 minutes), or until meat is no longer pink and a meat thermometer reads 160°. Brush tops with additional ketchup, if desired. Let stand 10 minutes before slicing.

Submitted by Linda Renninger – Dover International Speedway

Grilled Meatloaf Patties

That great meatloaf taste with the ease of a grilled hamburger.

2 pounds ground beef
1 egg, beaten
½ cup bread crumbs
½ cup grated cheese
¼ cup chopped onions
¼ cup steak sauce
¼ tablespoon pepper
Ketchup or steak sauce

Combine all ingredients except ketchup or steak sauce. Mix well and form into patties. I like to make the patties as square as possible. Grill over direct heat while basting lightly with the ketchup or steak sauce. You can also bake this dish at home, allow it to cool, slice, freeze, bring to the track and heat up on the grill using some foil.

Ground Beef Hash

2 pounds ground beef
1 (10¾-ounce) can cream of mushroom soup
1 large onion, minced
1 tablespoon oregano
1 teaspoon salt
1 teaspoon pepper
1 (16-ounce) can mixed veggies
1 (16-ounce) jar salsa

Brown ground beef; drain. Mix with remaining ingredients and simmer until thick. Serve with toast.

Submitted by Carol L. – Atlanta, GA – Jefferson Speedway

Jake Says—

Always bring a notepad, some pens or even an organizer (if you are serious about tailgate foods), to collect recipes, emails and phone numbers.

Morgan Shepherd

Driver – NASCAR
www.morganshepherd.com

How do you tell a future racecar driver at an early age? Look for the ten-year-old North Carolina kid rebuilding engines. Then when that same kid is learning to race on the back roads, you can be fairly sure the sport of racing is in his future.

Born in Ferguson, North Carolina, Morgan Shepherd was a winner only two years after launching his racing career in the Limited Sportsman Division. He won 21 of 29 races and the North Carolina Title. By 1980, Morgan had fine-tuned his racing skills, capturing second place and a national championship in NASCAR'S Late-Model Sportsman Division. Morgan soon returned to Cup racing and won his first Winston Cup victory at Martinsville, Viriginia in 1981.

In the years that followed, Morgan drove for several different Winston Cup car owners, including himself, Ray Mack Racing, Bud Moore Engineering, Wood Brothers, Butch Mack Motorsports, Precision Products Racing, Jasper Motorsports and more.

Today Morgan Shepherd Racing is supported by a few dedicated sponsors such as Red Line Oil and his fans. Morgan has put his faith and religion directly on the hood of his car. Besides his Victory in Jesus racing program, Morgan is also a core rider in the Kyle Petty Charity Ride, is active in the Race Against Drugs Program, as well as many other charities. He is also a dedicated husband and father. Talk about a great racing role model!

You can check out Morgan and even help sponsor a NEXTEL Cup team at www.morganshepherd.com.

PORK

Grilled Pork Roast with Pepper Jelly Glaze

This is my favorite recipe, and it's sooooo simple!

2 pounds pork loin roast

MARINADE:

½ cup apple juice
½ cup cider vinegar
½ cup hot pepper jelly

Place pork in large resealable plastic bag. Heat marinade ingredients together until jelly melts; pour over pork in bag. Seal bag; refrigerate 12–24 hours.

Remove pork from Marinade, discarding remaining Marinade. Place pork roast on medium-hot grill over drip pan; close grill hood. Grill pork about 1¼ hours, until meat thermometer inserted in center reads 150°.

GLAZE:

⅓ cup hot pepper jelly
2 tablespoons cider vinegar

Stir together Glaze ingredients; coat roast with jelly glaze. Grill 10 minutes more, bringing roast to an internal temperature of 160°. Let roast rest 10–15 minutes before slicing to serve. Serves 8.

Submitted by Anne L. Rehnstrom – The National Pork Board

Tammy's Pork Kabobs

- 2 tablespoons minced green pepper
- 2 tablespoons minced onion
- 1 tablespoon brown sugar
- ½ teaspoon dry ginger
- 1 garlic clove, crushed
- ½ cup soy sauce
- ¼ cup beer
- 1 whole pork tenderloin, cut into 6x½x⅛-inch strips

In medium bowl, stir together green pepper, onion, brown sugar, ginger, garlic, soy sauce and beer. Add pork, and cover. Make sure all of the pork gets a good coating. Keep in the fridge at least one hour or more. Place on skewers; cook over medium-high coals or gas. Add veggies as you desire.

Submitted by Tammy H. – Concord, N.C. – Dedicated Tony Stewart fan

Easy Citrus Pork Chops

I met Dan at a USAR Hooters Pro Cup race. His tailgating tip—"The simpler, the better! But don't skimp on the flavor."

- 4 pork chops
- 1 (8-ounce) can crushed pineapple
- 1 cup orange juice
- Dash of ginger
- Salt and pepper to taste

Place chops in a shallow baking pan, and top with pineapple, orange juice and a dash of ginger. Bake in a 325° oven about 1 hour. Sprinkle with salt and pepper before serving.

Submitted by Dan B. – Georgia

HEY RACE FANS, did you know that the first NASCAR-sanctioned event was held on Daytona's beach course February 15, 1948? That's just two months after Bill France, Sr. organized a meeting to discuss the forming of NASCAR. The NASCAR Series officially started June 19, 1949, when Jim Roper won a series race at the Charlotte, North Carolina, fairgrounds.

Southern "Cajun-Style" Pork Chops

5 or 6 bone-in pork chops
Salt and pepper to taste
Cajun seasoning
Oil
1 egg, beaten (or milk)
⅓ cup self-rising flour
⅓ cup self-rising cornmeal

Rinse your chops and sprinkle with salt, pepper and Cajun seasoning. Heat oil in a skillet. Place egg or milk in a dish. Combine cornmeal and flour in a separate dish. Dip chops in the beaten egg (or milk), and coat both sides with the cornmeal and flour mix. Place in the hot oil and cook until done. As soon as you pull the chops from the oil, sprinkle on some more Cajun seasoning "for good measure."

Submitted by Rick and Christy J. – Bristol race fans

Onion and Mushroom Pork Chops

This is easy and takes advantage of something that we're often short of at the track . . . time. This recipe can be made quicker than a ten-lap shootout!

4 pork chops
¼ cup lemon juice
Soy sauce
1 small onion, sliced
1 (10¾-ounce) can cream of mushroom soup, heated

Brush chops with lemon juice and soy sauce. Grill with onions until done, then top with hot cream of mushroom soup.

Submitted by Dan B. – Georgia

Salt 'n Pepper Beer Chops

You can use bone-in or boneless chops for this recipe.

Pork chops
Soy sauce
Salt and pepper
1 (12-ounce) can beer

Place chops on a plate and brush a light coat of soy sauce over both sides. Sprinkle salt and pepper over both sides and rub in gently.

Place chops on the grill and baste with beer while cooking. Turn as few times as possible.

Hickory Grilled Racetrack Ribs

2 racks pork ribs, membranes removed
Salt and pepper to taste (or lemon pepper)
½ cup apple cider vinegar
½ cup ketchup
¼ cup mustard
1 tablespoon lemon juice

Lay the ribs on a foil pan. Gently rub with some salt and pepper. Mix vinegar, ketchup, mustard and lemon juice. Baste the ribs completely. Using a few good-size hickory chunks and charcoal or hickory chips on your gas grill, set up for medium-high direct heat. Place ribs on the grill and cook about 10 minutes on bone side, then 10 minutes on meaty side. Re-baste and cook again until ribs brown evenly. Remove from the grill and place back into the foil pan. Add a bit of water or a dash of beer for extra moisture, if needed.

Cover the pan tightly with foil and move to a cooler area of the grill or reduce the heat to low. Cook an additional 2 hours. This will keep in the hickory taste and make your ribs very, very tender. Serve hot with a good basting of your favorite barbecue sauce.

Oriental Rib Tips

¾ cup soy sauce
1 tablespoon brown sugar
½ tablespoon ginger
½ tablespoon garlic powder
Frozen pork rib tips
Sesame seeds

Combine soy sauce, sugar, ginger and garlic powder. Marinate rib tips in the sauce. Remove from sauce, sprinkle with sesame seeds and place on the grill or smoker. Baste frequently with remaining sauce.

Memphis-Style Dry Rub Pork Ribs

4 pounds pork loin back ribs or meaty spareribs
1 tablespoon brown sugar
1 tablespoon paprika
1 tablespoon onion powder
¾ teaspoon celery salt
¾ teaspoon ground cumin
½ teaspoon black pepper
3 cups wood chips (use hickory or oak chips for the best flavor)

Cut ribs into 4 portions. Place in shallow dish. In small bowl, combine brown sugar, paprika, onion powder, celery salt, cumin and black pepper; rub evenly over meaty side of ribs. Cover with plastic wrap and marinate in the refrigerator 4–24 hours. At least 1 hour before grilling, soak wood chips in enough water to cover. Drain before using. In charcoal grill with a cover, place preheated coals around a drip pan for medium indirect heat. Add ½-inch hot water to drip pan.

Sprinkle half of the drained wood chips over the coals. Place ribs, bone side down, on grill rack over drip pan. Cover and grill for 1½–2 hours or until ribs are tender. Add more preheated coals (use a hibachi or a metal chimney starter to preheat coals) and wood chips; turn ribs halfway through grilling.

Submitted by the National Pork Board, proud sponsor of Frank Kimmel,
5-time ARCA RE/MAX Series champion
#46 Advance Auto Parts Ford
www.otherwhitemeat.com

Country-Style Ribs

1½–2 pounds boneless country-style ribs
2 cups apple cider vinegar
1 cup cold water
2 tablespoons vegetable oil
2 tablespoons molasses, or ¼ cup firmly packed brown sugar
1 tablespoon kosher salt
1½ teaspoons red pepper flakes
½ teaspoon cayenne pepper

Place ribs in a large bowl or resealable plastic bag; set aside. In 4-cup glass measure, stir together vinegar, water, oil, molasses, salt, red pepper flakes and cayenne pepper until salt is dissolved. Remove ½ cup marinade; set aside. Add remaining marinade to ribs; seal bag and marinate 4–6 hours in the refrigerator.

Remove ribs from marinade; discard marinade. Prepare medium-hot fire; grill ribs over indirect heat 50–60 minutes, or until pork is tender and the internal temperature reaches 160°. Baste ribs twice with reserved sauce mixture during last 15 minutes of grilling. Serves 6.

Serving Suggestions: Serve with hush puppies, corn on the cob, baked beans and your favorite corn bread.

Submitted by the National Pork Board, proud sponsor of Frank Kimmel,
5-time ARCA RE/MAX Series champion
#46 Advance Auto Parts Ford
www.otherwhitemeat.com

Frank Kimmel and his teammates anxiously wait for some great pork chops.

Frank Kimmel

Driver – ARCA, NASCAR, BUSCH, CRAFTSMAN
5-time ARCA RE/MAX Champion
Advance Auto Parts – National Pork Board #46 Ford Taurus

I first met Frank Kimmel at an ARCA RE/MAX race a few years back. When I was introduced to him, he stood up out of his camping chair, removed his glasses, shook my hand and offered me a cold soda and a barbecue sandwich. Now that's a guy I am going to root for during a race!

Frank started racing like most drivers, hitting local tracks in weekly series. He even won the championship at the Charleston Speedway in 1986–1987. He earned the championship at the Louisville Speedway in 1990. He moved around the NASCAR Series, the BUSCH Series as well as the Craftsman Truck Series and the NASCAR Winston West tour. Then came ARCA where Frank's skills and driving talent began to shine through.

"It helps your winning when you have a team behind you like I do, and great sponsors like Advance Auto Parts and the National Pork Board," Frank told me. "Not only does it help your winning numbers and racking up championships, but it also makes you a fan favorite. I have great fans in the stands."

Frank's fans are not only in the stands. At every ARCA RE/MAX race, the cooking crew from Smithfield Meats and the National Pork Board cook a few thousand pork sandwiches complete with Cookie's BBQ Sauce. "We always are a popular stop for members of other teams and people in the garage area."

NEAT THINGS ABOUT FRANK: 1992 ARCA Rookie of the Year. All-time ARCA RE/MAX money winner.

Easy Tangy Sweet Ribs

4 racks pork ribs
Salt and Pepper to taste
1 bottle favorite barbecue sauce
2 tablespoons hot pepper sauce
1 tablespoon honey
½ teaspoon garlic powder

After you remove the membrane from ribs, sprinkle with salt and pepper. Wrap in cling wrap and chill until needed. Mix barbecue sauce with remaining ingredients. Place ribs, bone side down, on grate of grill over medium heat. Cook, uncovered, for ½ hour; turn and cook an additional 30 minutes. Brush with some of the barbecue sauce every time you turn. You want to brown the outside of the ribs during the first turn, then reduce the heat some and continue to cook; turn and baste until meat is falling off the bone.

Oriental-Style Pork Steaks

All of my friends know how hard it is for me to pass up a Chinese buffet. So I came up with this version of a sweet and sour pork chop for a race-day cooking session.

1 chicken bouillon cube
¾ cup water
2 tablespoons vegetable or olive oil
4 pork steaks
¼ cup minced celery
1 tablespoon brown sugar
2 tablespoons soy sauce
1 tablespoon apple cider vinegar
1 tablespoon ginger
1 teaspoon mustard
Large dash of salt
Large dash of pepper
Sesame seeds (optional)

Dissolve bouillon cube in heated water. Heat a skillet; add oil and pork steaks. Cook until done. Remove from skillet, and quickly add remaining ingredients to same skillet. Reduce heat, stir and add chops back to mix. Serve whole or diced over noodles or rice.

Overnight Pork Casserole

1 pound sliced bacon
8 slices whole-wheat bread
6 eggs
1½ cups milk
1 cup (4 ounces) shredded Cheddar cheese
½ teaspoon dry mustard

Cut strips of bacon into ½-inch pieces. Cook in skillet over medium heat until crisp; blot with paper towels. Discard accumulated bacon fat. Remove crusts from bread, and reserve for another use. Cut bread slices into cubes; set aside. In a large bowl, beat eggs; stir in milk, cheese and mustard. Gently stir bacon and bread cubes into egg mixture; spoon into buttered 8-inch square baking dish. Cover tightly and refrigerate overnight.

Remove from refrigerator and let stand at room temperature for 15 minutes. Bake, uncovered, at 325° for 45 minutes or until knife inserted midway between center and outer edge comes out clean.

Submitted by the National Pork Board, proud sponsor of Frank Kimmel,
5-time ARCA RE/MAX Series champion
#46 Advance Auto Parts Ford
www.otherwhitemeat.com

Deck Chef Tip!

"Living high on the hog"

Do you know where that saying came from? It started among enlisted men in the U.S. Army, who received shoulder and leg cuts of pork while officers received the top loin cuts. So "living high on the hog" came to mean living well.

Italian Pork Steaks

6 pork steaks
1 cup Italian dressing
1 cup barbecue sauce

Place everything in a freezer bag and store in the fridge overnight. Cook on the grill at the track.

Dark Beer Brats

Brats
1–2 bottles dark beer
Onion powder
Garlic powder

Boil brats in beer, onion and garlic powder. When they puff up, move to the grill and grill until browned. Serve on a bun with your favorite toppings.

Submitted by Daniel R. – Race fan

Race-Day Kraut and Brats

Brats
1 (12-ounce) can beer
Water
1 onion, sliced
1 green pepper, sliced
2 tablespoons butter
1 tablespoon brown sugar
Bacon
Hot dog buns
Sauerkraut (optional)

Grill the brats enough to brown the outside. Poke a few holes in them, and toss them in a large pot with the beer and enough water to cover. Brown the onion and pepper in the butter and brown sugar. Wrap the drained brats in bacon and secure with a toothpick. Grill until bacon is done. Place on a bun; top with grilled veggies and even some sauerkraut, if desired.

Pit Stop Bratwurst

For some reason, bratwurst has become hard for people to cook. People are overthinking cooking a piece of sausage. Go figure! Here is a great way to cook a bratwurst that has that certain racing flair born straight from racetracks in the Carolinas.

1 package bratwurst
1 onion, sliced
1 bell pepper, sliced
1 (12-ounce) can beer
1 tablespoon brown sugar
½ cup barbecue sauce
Buns or rolls
Hot sauce (optional)

Combine all ingredients in a bowl, then cover. Chill for as long as possible. Remove bratwurst from marinade, and cook on a hot grill; heat the remaining marinade in a saucepan. Grill bratwursts until they plump up. Serve on a bun or French-style roll with heated sauce, onion and bell pepper. Add hot sauce, if desired.

Every team relies on the skills of the pit crew. During any race, they endure the blazing sun and fumes to be ready for that quick pit stop that could put their driver in the lead. That stop could last a brief fifteen seconds or less.

Grilled Smoked Sausage Packs

Instead of regular hot dogs and burgers, try these grilled smoked sausage packs.

1 (1-pound)package smoked sausage
1 onion, sliced
1 green pepper, sliced
1 bottle barbecue sauce
Hot dog buns

Combine sausage, onion and bell pepper in a foil pack, and cook over medium coals until done. Top with barbecue sauce and place on a bun.

Tailgate Grilled BBQ Kielbasa

1 pound (or more) kielbasa
Hot sauce
Barbecue sauce
Cheese
French bread buns, hard-style without seeds

Split the kielbasa into equal bun-length sections. Slice lengthwise almost in half. Coat with hot sauce, then grill, turning often and basting occasionally with barbecue sauce. When done, turn split side up and add cheese. Grill until the cheese melts, and serve on French bread buns.

Submitted by Daniel R. – Race fan

Hobo Dogs

A classic recipe from camping out as a kid still pops up around tailgate camps.

Hot dogs
1 can baked beans
1 small onion, sliced
Pre-cooked bacon strips

Prepare several sheets of foil, each about 12 inches long. Spray each sheet with nonstick spray (away from heat or open flame). Place a hot dog or two in the center of each piece of foil. Add a spoonfull of baked beans, a few onion slices and a slice of bacon. Gently fold over the foil and fold each open edge to seal as well as possible. Cook over medium-high heat and let the dog, beans and other ingredients simmer. Remove from heat, and place on a sturdy paper plate. Open the foil and dig in!

Brandon Miller, driver of the #21 Reese's Racing Chevrolet, brings his car down pit row for a qualifying run.

CHICKEN AND TURKEY

Michael Andretti's Grilled Chicken Quesadillas

Cooking oil
4 skinless boneless chicken breasts
8 flour tortillas
1 jar roasted red peppers, drained and thinly sliced
2 small green onions, thinly sliced
1½ cups shredded Monterey Jack cheese (or more)
2 baby portobello mushrooms, chopped
¾ cup chopped cilantro leaves

In a large frying pan, add enough oil to coat pan, then cook chicken until done. Remove and slice into strips. In another oiled skillet, place a tortilla in the pan and add 1 sliced chicken breast, ¼ of the peppers, ¼ of the green onions, ¼ of the cheese, some mushrooms and cilantro. Top with second tortilla. Cook for 2 minutes, then flip quesadilla and cook another 2 minutes. Slide quesadilla onto a plate or rack. Slice each into fourths or eighths, and serve with your favorite topping and a glass of Andretti Chardonnay.

Submitted by Michigan International Speedway / Michael Andretti
MIS Cookbook

HEY RACE FANS, did you know that in 2003, NASCAR recommended that teams use an alternate exit for the driver? This is commonly called a "roof hatch."

Steve's Spicy Asian Grilled Chicken

1 packet kung pao chicken seasoning
1 can coconut milk
½ teaspoon ginger
3 pounds chicken

Combine the seasoning, milk and ginger. Marinade the chicken cuts of your choice in the mix for as long as possible. Grill over medium-high heat. Baste as needed with remaining coconut mix. Serve hot with rice, as a sandwich or with veggies.

Submitted by A. N. – Dale Sr. fan

Tony's Pit Crew Grilled Oriental Chicken

Tony can cook up a storm! Try his Oriental Chicken. It's one of Tony's favorites.

4 boneless skinless chicken breasts
1 jar Naturally Fresh Oriental Salad Dressing, divided
1 (20-ounce) can sliced pineapple
2 bell peppers, cut into rings
1 pound cooked rice

Using a dinner plate, press the chicken breasts to a uniform thickness. Marinate the chicken breasts 4 hours in ⅔ jar salad dressing.

Grill chicken over hot coals (or medium-high flame) on one side for 7 minutes. Turn, and top each with a pineapple slice and 2 pepper slices. Brush on or drizzle with the remaining salad dressing. Cover the grill and cook for 7 minutes or until the chicken is done. Serve over a bed of rice.

Submitted by Tony Taffar – Gasman / Cook
#16 Naturally Fresh USAR Hooters Pro Cup Series

Brandon Knupp

Driver – ARCA RE/MAX, ARCA Truck
www.brandonknupp.com

Brandon has been driving since he was nine years old. "I am a rookie who has been driving forever!" Brandon said with a smile in his hauler before a race. So how does a kid from Sidney, Ohio, get into racing?

According to Brandon, it was fairly simple. "My dad asked if I wanted to do it. I said HECK YEAH! And I guess that was it. He was into cars and so we started with go-kart racing, local stuff." That was when Brandon was nine and says, "I have been doing it ever since . . . and having fun!"

Brandon started in go-karts, then hit the trucks and ARCA cars and even sprint cars. I asked him what the difference is between the stock car he is now driving and his sprint car. "This thing is like a tank! It's a lot more like driving, you have to be in control of your ride."

Being a driver means Brandon eats a lot of food cooked in the infield or on the road. I asked him what his favorite foods were and the answers were almost as in-depth as his answers to racing questions.

FAVORITE FOOD: I always want some good barbecue when I am at the track or at a race party or cookout. On race days, I eat light and drink lots of water. But when I have the time to sit down and enjoy it, I really like Italian.

Anthony's Orange Juice Chicken

4 chicken breasts
¼ teaspoon black pepper
1 tablespoon olive oil
⅓ cup orange juice
2 teaspoons vinegar
2 green onions, diced
1 tablespoon minced onion
½ tablespoon minced garlic

Combine everything in a zip-close bag, and freeze before you head to the track. Thaw and grill until done, basting occasionally with the sauce.

Submitted by Anthony C. – Tony Stewart fan

Chicken Stuffed Baked Potatoes

Taters are cheap and easy to cook. Here is a tasty stuffed one for a very filling speedway meal.

5–6 large baking potatoes
Minced garlic
3 chicken breasts, or 6 tenders
Barbecue sauce
1 cup real bacon bits
1 large onion, diced
2 cups grated Cheddar cheese
Sour cream

Wrap the taters in foil and bake in an oven or place on a covered grill. When the taters get close, about 15 minutes from being done, place the chicken on the grill and cook until done.

Remove chicken and shred with a fork. Stir in a healthy amount of barbecue sauce. Add bacon bits, onion and any spices you might like; mix well. Carefully remove taters from the grill, slice open and add equal amounts of the chicken topping to each. Cover with cheese and place on the grill for a few minutes to melt cheese. You could keep the taters whole or divide into halves and serve that way. Serve hot topped with sour cream.

Honey Orange Chicken Breasts

A very easy chicken recipe that can be baked or grilled to your liking!

4 boneless skinless chicken breast halves
Salt and pepper to taste
½ cup honey mustard
1 tablespoon ground ginger
1 tablespoon minced garlic
¼ cup orange marmalade

Clean and rinse chicken breasts. Apply a very light coating of salt and pepper over the chicken, and gently rub in. Combine the remaining items, and marinate the chicken in the mix for several hours. Grill or bake until done. Baste with remaining sauce while cooking.

Hint: Try cutting the cooked chicken into strips and serving over a salad.

Deck Chef Tip!

Time to marinate

At least a thirty-minute marinating time is needed to add rich flavor. But a simple rule of thumb is to remember that the cheaper the steak, the longer the marinating time. Cheaper steaks are often tougher cuts with less fatty tissue.

Easy Jamaican Jerk Chicken

2 red onions, minced
2 green peppers, minced
2 tablespoons cayenne pepper
1/4 cup ground ginger
1/4 cup Cajun seasoning
1 tablespoon cinnamon
Salt and pepper to taste
3 cups olive oil
1 1/2 cups white vinegar
1 1/2 cups soy sauce
4–5 boneless chicken breasts or tenders

Mix everything together, and marinate in a freezer bag overnight. You can even freeze the chicken in the bag and take it to the track to be cooked.

Cook over medium-high heat on the grill (thaw if frozen); use with kabobs or chicken on a stick. Baste as you cook with remaining sauce.

Tailgate Chicken Parmesan

Here is a great and SO EASY recipe for Chicken Parmesan—well suited for RV campers and tailgaters. It is perfect for a small oven, and can be done on a covered grill.

4–6 boneless chicken breasts
1 egg, beaten
3/4 cup bread crumbs
2 tablespoons Italian seasoning
1/4 cup Parmesan cheese
1 tablespoon garlic powder
1 can or jar pizza sauce
1 cup mozzarella cheese

Rinse chicken. Dip in beaten egg, then roll in combined bread crumbs, Italian seasoning, and garlic powder; sprinkle with Parmesan cheese. Cook uncovered in a 350° oven 15–20 minutes. Top with sauce, and cook about 10 minutes more. Top with mozzarella cheese, and cook until cheese is melted. Serve with hot noodles.

Easy Tex-Mex Grilled Chicken

A simple and tasty recipe perfect for a Texas race-day grilling session.

4–6 chicken breasts
Lemon juice
1 pack taco seasoning
Grated cheese

Rinse chicken breasts; while they are still moist, squirt on some lemon juice. Rub taco seasoning evenly over each piece. You can grill or bake this. I prefer to grill over medium-high direct heat. When done, serve with grated cheese on a bun or over salad greens.

Grilled Spicy Mushroom Chicken

This recipe is perfect for any cut of chicken, and perfect for your tailgate grilling needs.

1 (5-pound) bag frozen chicken thighs
1 stick butter
1 cup Cajun seasoning
1 ($10\frac{3}{4}$-ounce) can cream of mushroom soup

Place chicken in a large pot. Cover with water, add butter and bring to a boil. Stir gently to make sure chicken cooks evenly. Remove each piece of chicken and roll in Cajun seasoning until covered well. Grill until browned. Before removing from grill, baste with cream of mushroom soup. Serve hot.

HEY RACE FANS, did you know that the father of brothers Rusty Wallace, Kenny Wallace and Mike Wallace was one of the most successful short track drivers in the Midwest?

Kenny Wallace

Driver – NASCAR, BUSCH, ASA
www.kennywallace.com

Kenny Wallace, often voted most popular driver, is known as being the funny guy around the pits and garage area. Here he takes time to visit with fans.

Kenny Wallace is one of the funniest and friendliest people I have ever met. But what struck me about Kenny is the fact that he is also one of the most serious people I have ever met. Kenny is serious about his family, his kids, friends, and of course racing. "People tell me all the time how hard I had it getting to where I am now. I look at it as how lucky I am to have had this chance. I've worked hard, and my wife has worked hard. My whole family has worked hard in this industry. Who says you can't have a good time when you are doing it? You only have one chance. You might as well enjoy it."

Kenny, nicknamed Herman by one of his father's friends when he was growing up, learned to drive like any kid. "My dad Russ would take me down to Mr. Miller's car dealership. I used to spend hours a day in a showroom behind the wheel of every new car running races in my mind. The whole time my father and his friends were solving the world's problems over a good conversation. There was a comic character at the time named Herman the German or something . . . not too smart. Mr. Miller would shout out, "What has Herman done?"

Cheese-Topped Chicken Taco Pie

1 frozen 9-inch pie crust

Heat oven to 450°; bake crust 9–11 minutes or until light golden brown. Before filling shell, place in a 10-inch pie plate to prevent overflow into oven when baking.

FILLING:

2 cups chopped, cooked chicken
1 package taco seasoning mix
1 (16-ounce) jar chunky salsa
1 (2.8-ounce) can French fried onions (Cheddar ones are good), divided
1 cup ricotta cheese
1 (8-ounce) package (2 cups) shredded taco-flavored cheese blend
2 eggs, beaten
1 small tomato, seeded, diced

Reduce heat to 350°. Place cooked chicken in skillet; stir in taco seasoning and salsa. Bring to a boil. Reduce heat; simmer uncovered 5 minutes, stirring occasionally. Add half the French fried onions; mix well. Spoon mixture into baked crust.

In a small bowl, combine ricotta cheese, 1 cup taco-flavored cheese blend and eggs; mix well. Spoon over chicken mixture. Bake at 350° for 25–35 minutes or until slightly puffed and set in center.

Remove pie from oven. Sprinkle remaining 1 cup cheese evenly over Filling. Top with remaining French fried onions. Return to oven; bake an additional 2–3 minutes or until cheese is melted. Sprinkle tomatoes around edge and in center. Let pie stand 10 minutes before serving.

Note: Can be made with 1 pound ground beef rather than chicken.

Submitted by Linda Renninger – Dover International Speedway

Lemon Pepper Chicken Thighs

1 bag frozen chicken thighs
1 cup olive oil
1 tablespoon minced garlic
1 cup lemon juice
2 tablespoons pepper
1 tablespoon dried rosemary

If available, find frozen chicken thighs in a resealable zip-close bag. If not just use some large freezer bags. The night before cooking, combine all of the ingredients, including frozen chicken thighs, in the bag. Reseal and place into the fridge, not the freezer. Stand up so your bag won't leak.

Allow the chicken to completely thaw in the mixture. Remove from the bag and cook on the grill. Baste with a bit of butter, if desired.

Jake Says—

For the price, you can't beat a few large bags of chicken thighs. You can cook them just about any way you like and won't have to feel stingy about giving a few away.

Teriyaki Chicken Thighs

Sesame seeds
1 cup soy sauce
1 cup grapefruit juice
1/4 cup ketchup
1/4 cup rice wine vinegar
1/4 cup brown sugar
1 tablespoon minced garlic
3 tablespoons ground ginger
Thawed chicken thighs

Combine all of the ingredients, and marinate the thighs as long as possible, covered, in the fridge. Grill until done, and serve hot.

Submitted by Rebecca and Charles – NASCAR fans and campers

Sweet Dijon Grilled Chicken

1/2 cup olive oil
1/2 cup white Zinfandel
3 tablespoons Dijon mustard
2 tablespoons honey or maple syrup
2 teaspoons minced garlic
1 teaspoon ground black pepper
1/2 teaspoon salt
Dash of paprika
3 pounds chicken thighs or breasts

In a bowl, combine all of the ingredients except chicken. Coat the chicken well and store in zip-close bags. I suggest doing this the night before cooking. You can freeze, if needed. Grill over medium-high heat and baste with remaining marinade. Sprinkle a bit of paprika over the chicken before removing from the grill.

Blazing Hot Chicken Thighs

According to Stan, he used to buy chicken tenders by the "ton" and cook them all of the time. "Now I buy chicken thighs or drums because you can feed a bunch more people." Here is Stan's recipe for some HOT chicken thighs!

2 cups jalepeño peppers
1 (8-ounce) can crushed pineapple
2 cups apple cider vinegar
2 tablespoons minced garlic
½ tablespoon olive oil
1 teaspoon salt
1 teaspoon pepper
2 bags frozen thighs, drums, etc.

Combine all of the ingredients, and cover the chicken as much as possible. Cover and place in the bottom of the fridge, overnight if possible. Don't grill until chicken is thawed completely. Grill until done; baste with sauce.

Submitted by Stan F. – 'Bama race fan

Bodine escapes a fire-filled car after making contact with the wall along the front stretch. He was not injured in the wreck. The car is a different story.

Almost Cheating Smoked Turkey Legs

Here is a way you can bring some smoked turkey flavor to your race-day tailgate without having to haul a smoker.

Assorted smoked turkey pieces still on the bone with skin
Butter
Black pepper
Barbecue sauce

Place the turkey in water to cover in a large bowl to add some moisture. Remove the legs and rub down with a very light coat of butter; sprinkle on some black pepper. Wrap in foil and place on the grill to heat up. When properly heated remove from foil and apply some of your favorite barbecue sauce. Allow to grill for a few more minutes. The turkey meat will fall off the bone!

JASON JARRET'S TIP: Be careful when frying a turkey. Fill the pot with water first to see how much oil you will need.

Christina and Jason Jarrett

ARCA Series
#25 Central Merchant Services Chevrolet
www.jasonjarett.com

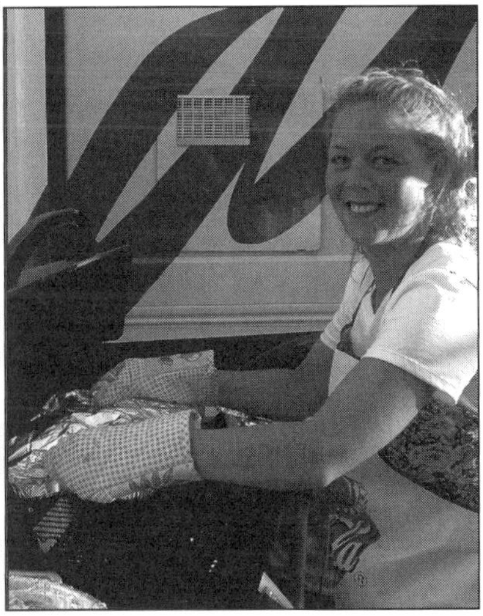

While Jason Jarret stands out in front of the motor coach cooking a huge fried turkey and talking to friends the day before his next race, his wife Christina is busy cooking just about everything else. "I started cooking for the team about a season ago and now it has turned into a business." And judging by the reaction of the crew and friends, the business is good!

"I like to try new things, but keep it simple as well," Christina said. "Simple, but fast paced!" While talking to Christina, she went back and forth between the motor coach kitchen and the grill outside with the skill and speed of a pit crew! Like anything at a racetrack during a race weekend, timing is very important. Crews have to be here, there, and then back here. Then drivers have meetings, cars to get checked, and somewhere along the line, a race takes place. "While all of that is going on, they still have to eat," Christina said.

And eat they do. During my visit, the spread Christina put on the table was impressive, as was the fried turkey. And you could tell by the line of crew members standing with plates in their hands, the fantastic meal was well appreciated.

Jason, son of Dale Jarrett and grandson of Ned Jarrett, has raced in just about every series: Go-karts, NASCAR Late Model, ARCA RE/MAX, NASCAR BUSCH and NASCAR NEXTEL.

CHRISTINA'S TIP: Find new recipes and try them. Keep it fresh!

Grilled Speedway Turkey

This is a pretty simple recipe that requires you do a bit of pre-cooking before the turkey hits the fire, but it is worth it. You could do the boiling at home, freeze the turkey and grill at the track. But it's better if done all the same day. If using a gas grill, some wood chips or pellets would add some great flavor.

2 beers
1 stick butter
¼ cup orange juice
1 tablespoon black pepper
Large dash of salt
Barbecue sauce
Assorted turkey pieces (or chicken)

Bring beer and butter to a boil. Add orange juice, pepper and salt. Add enough water to completely cover meat. Boil turkey (or chicken) until done. Gently remove as not to pull meat away from bones. Place the meat on a hot grill and baste with your favorite barbecue sauce.

Grilled Turkey or Ham Roll Up

This is a version of a recipe I tried at a dirt track. The lady was on one of those low-carb diets, but did not want to eat all of the bacon and sausage and stuff. She would buy deli meat sliced real thick and make some great grilled roll ups.

Thick-sliced deli turkey or ham
Swiss cheese, sliced thin
Dijon mustard
Cajun seasoning

Top each slice of meat with a slice of Swiss cheese. You can add onion, veggies, hot peppers or whatever, if desired. Roll up and secure roll with a toothpick. Spread a very thin coat of mustard, just enough for flavor, on the outside of the roll. Place on the grill and grill until cheese melts and there are grill marks on the meat. Sprinkle with Cajun seasoning.

SEAFOOD

Cajun Tilapia with Honey Butter Sauce

I suggested this quick and tasty recipe to a tailgater I met at a race. Fried fish was wearing out and he had started a diet and wanted to lose the breading and oil. Cook in an oven or covered grill.

4 tilapia fillets (fresh or frozen)
2 tablespoons melted butter
1 teaspoon hot sauce
1 teaspoon honey
½ teaspoon minced garlic
2 tablespoons Cajun seasoning

Lay fillets on a well-greased oven pan. Melt butter; add hot sauce, honey and garlic. Brush butter mixture over fillets, and bake about 20 minutes in a 350° oven. Before removing, sprinkle with Cajun seasoning and cook about 5 more minutes. Fish is done when it flakes easily with a fork. I top mine with a blend of sautéed veggies. Serve with tartar sauce.

Pan-Fried Hot Fish

A good piece of Hot Fish is worth its weight in tartar sauce! A Southern favorite, this recipe is perfect for a cast-iron skillet.

2 pounds fish fillets
½ cup yellow cornmeal
½ cup all-purpose flour
2 tablespoons steak sauce
2 tablespoons hot sauce
1 teaspoon salt
1 teaspoon pepper
Cooking oil

If using frozen fish, allow pieces to thaw. In a large bowl, mix cornmeal and flour together. Rub fish fillets all over with steak sauce, hot sauce, salt and pepper. Gently roll each piece in the cornmeal and flour mix. In a skillet, heat oil until very hot. Carefully place fish in the skillet and quickly brown each side for about 2 minutes. Then cook each side for an additional 2 minutes if needed, depending on how thick your fish is. Serve hot with tarter sauce on a bun or with a side of chips.

Rum Grilled Tilapia

This is a very simple dish. It only takes a few minutes to prepare, and depending on the thickness of the fillet, only a few minutes to grill. I suggest using a grill grate cover with small holes so your fish won't fall apart. You can also use heavy-duty foil. Apply a very thin coat of oil to keep it from sticking.

8 tilapia fillets
¼ cup rum
1 lemon
Parsley flakes
Paprika
Salt and pepper to taste

Rub a little olive oil or veggie oil all over fillets to help keep from sticking. Turn fish skin side down and gently drizzle some rum on each piece. Rub it over the fish to spread it out. Squirt lemon juice on each piece and sprinkle with parsley, paprika, salt and pepper. Cook on the grill, skin side down. Cook until fish flakes easily. Serve hot.

Deck Chef Tip!

Great Fish!

Want to grill some great fish? Try a hinged wire seafood grilling basket. These are great for cooking whole fish such as snapper, trout or salmon. It also works well for fillets of smaller, more tender fish.

Grilled Fish Packets

2–3 fish fillets
1 onion, sliced
1 green pepper, sliced
Lemon juice
Salt, pepper and Cajun seasoning to taste
White wine
Butter

Top each fillet with equal portions of onion and pepper slices on a piece of foil. Sprinkle with lemon juice, spices, wine and butter. Fold the foil packet so no steam can escape. Grill over medium-high heat about 4 minutes each side. Fish is done when it flakes easily with a fork or knife.

Submitted by Ryan and Cole – Kentucky Speedway / BUSCH fans

Tony's Seafood Delight

2–4 garlic cloves
1 medium onion
1 bell pepper
½ stick butter
1 pound shrimp, peeled
1 pack imitation crabmeat
1 cup frozen peas and carrots
½ cup diced ham
1 jar Alfredo sauce
½ cup white wine or sherry
Pasta
Parmesan
Salt, pepper and spices to taste

Finely chop garlic, onion and pepper. Sauté in butter until tender. Add the shrimp and sauté until all shrimp are pink. Add the crab, vegetables and ham. Cook 3–5 minutes. Stir in the Alfredo sauce and wine. Cook until the sauce is hot. Serve over any pasta. Top with Parmesan cheese. Season with salt, pepper and any spices to taste. All ingredients and amounts are only suggestions.

Submitted by Tony Taffar – Gasman/Cook
#16 Naturally Fresh USAR Hooters Pro Cup Series

Butter Grilled Scallops

Use your grill and a foil pan to make some great grilled scallops at the track.

1 pound scallops
Butter or olive oil
Soy sauce
Cajun seasoning

Place a foil pan over medium heat. Place scallops and butter or olive oil in the pan. Brown scallops on all edges. Add soy sauce and sprinkle with Cajun seasoning as desired. Serve hot with rice or a favorite side.

Submitted by Katie D. – Jasper, GA – Dale, Sr. and Dale, Jr. fan

Tailgate Gumbo

"If I leave out the okra, I toss in some rice and extra butter and it's then jambalaya." I like Terry's thinking.

1 cup flour
1 cup oil
1 package frozen sliced okra
4 cups water
3 chicken bouillon cubes
1 (10-ounce) can tomatoes and diced chiles
3 tablespoons Cajun seasoning
½ tablespoon minced garlic
1 teaspoon salt
1 teaspoon pepper
½ teaspoon ground bay leaves
2 cups diced or canned chicken
2 cups sliced smoked sausage
1 small package frozen bite-size shrimp
Hot sauce (optional)

Terry suggests making the roux (the oil and flour mix) at home before the tailgate. But here is the recipe. Over medium-high heat in a saucepan, combine the flour and the oil. Cook until the flour mixture turns brown. In a large pot, combine the remaining ingredients, including your roux, and simmer until the gumbo thickens. Add in some extra Cajun seasoning and a dash of hot sauce, if you like.

Submitted by Terry – ASA race fan

Shrimp and Grits

1½ pounds shrimp, peeled
1 pound bacon
1 large onion, chopped
Flour
Salt and pepper to taste
Milk
Deluxe Grits (see recipe page 34)

Boil shrimp and save the water; set boiled shrimp aside. Fry bacon, remove from grease and crumble. Sauté onion in bacon grease. Add flour to grease and onions to make a roux. (If you need more grease, add a stick of butter or some shortening.) After flour browns, add some salt and pepper. Pour in some milk and shrimp water and cook until it reaches the right consistency for gravy. Add shrimp to gravy and stir well Serve over Deluxe Grits.

Submitted by Tony Taffar – Gasman/Cook
#16 Naturally Fresh USAR Hooters Pro Cup Series

Jeff Gordon edges out the #32 car as the fans cheer him on.

Macee's Popcorn Shrimp

My son loves popcorn shrimp. Here is a simple way to make popcorn shrimp with a bit of kick. Try it as a dish by itself or for a perfect shrimp po' boy sandwich.

1 pound small shrimp, peeled and cleaned
½ cup flour
½ cup cornmeal
1 cup beer
¼ cup sugar
1 egg
¼ cup Cajun seasoning
¼ cup minced onion
1 tablespoon garlic powder
Oil for frying
Cajun seasoning

Rinse shrimp. Combine all of the remaining ingredients. Pour rinsed shrimp into the batter. Add more beer or even milk, if needed. Place batter-covered shrimp into hot oil and cook until golden brown. As soon as you remove them from the oil, sprinkle with Cajun seasoning. Serve hot.

Grilled Shrimp and Vegetables

Tony loves cooking and working as a team member for a USAR Hooters Pro Cup Series car. Tony says, "Unlike the set rules for pit stops, cooking can be a bit easier. I use recipes as guidelines, and when I see something I would do differently, I fix it MY way." Follow Tony's advice; have fun with your cooking and try some new things.

1 pound large shrimp, peeled and deveined
2 bell peppers, cut into chunks
1 onion, quartered
Whole fresh mushrooms
Salt and pepper to taste
1 jar Naturally Fresh Ranch Salad Dressing

Alternate shrimp and vegetables on a skewer. Season to taste. Brush with the salad dressing. Grill 10–15 minutes over medium heat. Brush often with salad dressing.

Submitted by Tony Taffar – Gasman/Cook
#16 Naturally Fresh USAR Hooters Pro Cup Series

Cajun Butter Grilled Shrimp

You can use this butter recipe on just about anything from corn to shrimp. I tend to like the stuff on grilled shrimp!

GARLIC BUTTER:

½ cup butter
1 teaspoon Worcestershire sauce
1 tablespoon lemon juice
1 tablespoon hot sauce
1 teaspoon minced garlic
1 teaspoon Cajun seasoning
Black pepper

Combine all and mix in a saucepan.

2 pounds jumbo shrimp, shelled and deveined
1 lemon cut in half
Pineapple slices (optional)

Melt Garlic Butter in saucepan and allow to cool. Place shrimp in one or two zip-close bags and pour in Garlic Butter mixture. MAKE SURE IT'S COOL. Press out excess air, seal and tumble in your hands to coat every piece. Keep chilled until ready to grill. Place on skewers, squeeze on lemon juice, and grill with some pineapple slices, if desired.

Everything in today's racing world is watched by safety officials. Notice the official to the left. He is watching the pit crew to ensure no safety violations happen during the pit stop. Teams can be penalized during a race or even fined after a race if something goes wrong during a pit stop.

Tony Taffer

Pit Crew Gasman – USAR Hooters Pro Cup #16 Naturally Fresh Ford Taurus

During a conversation with some of the great people at Naturally Fresh Dressings about the Naturally Fresh racing programs, I was told that I had to meet the gasman, Tony. So when the chance came up, Tony and I sat down and talked about two great subjects, racing and cooking!

Cooking comes from the heart with Tony. When he first moved away from home, he realized how much he missed home cooking. "I did what I had to do. I called home and asked my mom!" This led to countless hours in the kitchen at home as well as in the United States Navy and later working for a Nuclear Plant. "I often cooked in the navy and worked third shift at work and became the shift chef."

I asked Tony what foods would be considered favorites when people come by his kitchen for dinner. "I do a very good teriyaki chicken. I also like grilling shrimp and vegetables. I would love to get better at baking."

After talking about food, the conversation turned to racing. "I love this sport. I lived in Dawnsonville, Georgia, and now in South Carolina. Racing is everywhere!" Next time you see Tony, ask him about racing and pit crews, then toss in a question about marinades and seasonings. He can answer them all.

Tailgate Cajun Shrimp Boil

2 packages frozen half ears corn
4 large potatoes, cubed
½ (12-ounce) can beer
2 tablespoons sugar
1 bottle hot sauce (or to taste)
Water to cover
½ cup Cajun seasoning (or to taste)
2–3 pounds medium shrimp

Bring all ingredients (except shrimp) to a boil. Cook until potatoes are done. Add shrimp and cook until shrimp turn pink. Serve hot.

Submitted by the Scott Family – North Carolina
Lowes Motor Speedway fans

Shrimp Burgers

Tony, a member of the Naturally Fresh #16 USAR Hooters Pro Cup pit crew, is an incredible cook. He brags about these Shrimp Burgers, and shares his secret recipe.

1 pound boiled shrimp, peeled
½ onion, chopped
1 bell pepper, chopped
1 egg, beaten
1 cup bread crumbs
1 (2-ounce) jar chopped pimentos
1 tablespoon Old Bay Seafood Seasoning
¼ cup milk
¼ cup flour (or more)

Use a potato masher to mash the shrimp. Leave some big pieces. Stir in the next 7 ingredients. Add ¼ cup flour, adding more if needed to make a consistency that will hold together. Make patties like a hamburger. Fry in shallow oil in a frying pan. Turn after the first side is browned. Serve on hamburger buns with mayonnaise and cocktail sauce.

Submitted by Tony Taffar – Gasman/Cook
#16 Naturally Fresh USAR Hooters Pro Cup Series

Coconut Shrimp

1 egg, beaten
¾ cup all-purpose flour, divided
½ (12-ounce) can beer
1½ teaspoons baking powder
½ tablespoon ginger
2 cups flaked coconut
24 shrimp, peeled, tails on
Oil for frying

In a bowl, mix egg, ½ cup flour, beer and baking powder. In a separate bowl, mix remaining ¼ cup flour and ginger; put the coconut in another bowl. Coat shrimp in flour/ginger mixture. Dip in the batter, then roll in coconut. Cook in hot oil, turning as little as possible. Cook until golden brown.

Katie's Shrimp Kabobs

Katie will set you straight on the best drivers in racing—"Dale Earnhart, Sr. and Dale Earnhart, Jr." She will also set you straight on how to make one fine shrimp kabob. Here is Katie's favorite race-day recipe.

30 jumbo shrimp, boiled
2 chicken breasts, or 6 chicken tenders
2 apples, sliced
1 pint cherry tomatoes
1 (20-ounce) can pineapple chunks, juice reserved
Squeeze butter
2 tablespoons brown sugar

Peel and clean shrimp. Clean, rinse and cube chicken. Alternate shrimp, chicken, apples, tomatoes, and pineapple on skewers. Baste in butter and place over medium-high heat. In another saucepan, combine brown sugar, reserved pineapple juice and more butter. Bring to a boil, remove from heat and baste kabobs often. Cook until chicken is browned and shrimp turn pink. Serve hot.

Submitted by Katie D. – Jasper, GA – Dale, Sr. and Dale, Jr. fan

HEY RACE FANS, did you know that the Dodge/Save Mart 350 NASCAR Winston Cup event at Infineon is one of the few on the Winston Cup schedule measured in kilometers? This event is 110 laps, or 220 miles or 354.2 kilometers.

SAUCES, RUBS AND MARINADES

Carolina-Style Vinegar Sauce

2 cups water
1 cup apple cider vinegar
3 tablespoons crushed red pepper
1 tablespoon black pepper
1 tablespoon minced garlic
Salt and pepper to taste

Mix all ingredients in a jar, and place in the fridge for a couple of days. Goes well with salad greens, cold veggies or meat and fish dishes.

Submitted by Alan N. – NHRA fan

Orange Aioli Sauce

This is a great sauce to use as a spread on a sandwich bun.

1 cup mayonnaise
¼ cup orange juice
1 tablespoon hot pepper sauce
½ teaspoon sugar
½ teaspoon minced garlic
½ teaspoon prepared horseradish
2 tablespoons chopped scallions
Dash of salt
Dash of pepper

Stir all ingredients together, and refrigerate until ready to use. Popular accompaniment for fish, meats and veggies.

Hollandaise Sauce

3 egg yolks
1 tablespoon cold water
¼ teaspoon salt
1 teaspoon lemon or lime juice
½ cup butter, melted

If possible, use a blender or mixer to combine the egg yolks, water, salt and lemon or lime juice, and mix about 20 seconds or less. Heat the butter to boiling, and slowly add to the egg mixture as you blend. Mix until the sauce begins to thicken. Serve immediately over eggs Benedict (see page 31), or use to embellish veggies or fish.

Submitted by Sheri "The Chef" and Foster – BUSCH Series fans

Easy Shrimp Cocktail Sauce

1 cup ketchup
½ cup mild taco sauce
1 tablespoon lemon juice
1 tablespoon Worcestershire sauce
1 teaspoon horseradish sauce
Dash of garlic

Mix all, chill and serve with shrimp.

Deck Chef Tip!

Play it safe

Cooking at the racetrack can cause a few problems with sauces. Sauces that use creams or eggs should be used as quickly as possible or kept chilled. To easily keep your signature sauce, store it in a squeeze bottle on ice until needed.

Tailgate Tartar Sauce

Perfect with fried fish during your next tailgate. Also great on a po' boy sandwich. Just make sure you chill it good and keep it cold.

2 cups mayo
3 tablespoons sweet pickle relish
2 tablespoons hot sauce
1 teaspoon lemon juice
1 teaspoon paprika

Combine ingredients well, and serve cold.

Cajun Seafood Tartar Sauce

This is a very nice (and SPICY) version of a tartar sauce. According to Angie, this sauce makes her husband's fried fish sandwiches perfect.

1½ cups mayo
1 cup hot salsa
½ cup hot sauce
2 tablespoons minced onion
1 tablespoon crushed red pepper
1 tablespoon minced garlic
1 tablespoon Cajun seasoning
Lemon or lime juice

Combine and chill. Serve over a fish fillet on a French roll.

Submitted by Carter and Angie C. – NASCAR / BUSCH / ARCA fans

Hot Butter Dipping Sauce

1 stick butter
1 teaspoon lemon pepper seasoning
1 tablespoon hot sauce
½ teaspoon brown sugar

Combine all ingredients in a saucepan and melt over medium heat. Use as a dipping sauce for shrimp, seafood, bread, etc.

Submitted by Andy B. – Nashville, TN

Honey Butter Drizzle Sauce

This recipe is straight from Lowe's Motor Speedway. Thanks to Eric for showing me how to make it while frying chicken and listening to practice times on his scanner.

½ cup minced onion
1 tablespoon minced garlic
2 tablespoons butter
2 lemon slices
½ cup butter, melted
½ cup honey
Dash of salt and pepper
Hot sauce (optional)

Brown onion and garlic in butter in a skillet. Reduce heat and squeeze lemon juice into mixture. Add remaining ingredients. Let cool for a few minutes to thicken some. Drizzle over fried chicken wings, etc.

Jake Says—

Mix 2 parts peanut butter with 1 part honey. Keep in a sealed container and serve with crackers, apple slices or bananas for a quick snack.

Quick and Easy Barbeque Sauce

Looking for a good sauce that is easy to make and filled with flavor? Try this recipe given to me at the USAR Hooters race in Jefferson, Georgia.

1½ cups ketchup
⅓ cup lemon juice
½ cup cider vinegar
2 tablespoons brown sugar
¼ cup Worcestershire sauce
½ tablespoon mustard
Large dash of cumin powder

Combine everything in a saucepan, and simmer about 20 minutes.

Submitted by J. D. – USAR Hooters Pro Cup racing team member

Bill's Camping BBQ Sauce

1 large onion, chopped
2 pieces bacon
2 tablespoons minced garlic
1 tablespoon bacon drippings
2 tablespoons Worcestershire sauce
1 bottle ketchup
⅓ cup apple cider vinegar

Brown onion, bacon and garlic in bacon drippings; add Worcestershire sauce. Break the bacon into tiny pieces as it cooks. Stir in ketchup and vinegar. Simmer a few minutes, then remove from heat.

Submitted by Bill R., Jr. – NHRA fan

Cold Cola Barbecue Sauce

This recipe has many versions. But this one has a bit of extra zest that is sure to make a great sauce.

1 (12-ounce) can cola (not diet)
1 cup ketchup
1 small onion, minced
2 tablespoons apple cider vinegar
2 tablespoons soy sauce
2 tablespoons mustard
1 tablespoon horseradish sauce

Combine ingredients in a saucepan, and simmer about 15 minutes.

Kent's Strawberry Barbecue Sauce

I hosted a chef demo at the outdoor Chattanooga Market the same weekend as a nearby strawberry festival, so I came up with this sauce recipe. The next weekend, I served it to some appreciative race fans.

1 cup fresh strawberries
½ cup minced celery
½ cup minced onion
½ cup minced green pepper
1 tablespoon minced japaleño pepper
1 garlic clove, minced
½–1 cup honey
⅓ cup apple cider vinegar
⅔ cup ketchup or tomato sauce
1 teaspoon cumin powder

Purée strawberries. Combine all ingredients in a saucepan and simmer.

Texas-Style Barbecue Sauce

1 (10-ounce) bottle Worcestershire sauce
1 (12-ounce) can beer
½ cup ketchup
½ cup apple cider vinegar
½ cup minced onion
¼ cup minced jalapeño pepper
3 tablespoons lemon juice
3 tablespoons brown sugar
2 tablespoons minced garlic
1 stick butter, melted

Combine all of the ingredients in a saucepan and bring to a boil. Reduce heat and simmer about 10 minutes.

Submitted by Juan and Suzie – Texas Motor Speedway campers

Cathy Venturini

Billy Venturini Racing
www.billyventurini.com

For years Cathy followed her husband Bill Venturini from track to track while he racked up a bunch of wins including two ARCA Series driving championships. "We've been around here a while," Cathy said. Now their son Billy carries on the driving legacy of the family while Cathy is the team owner and Bill is the crew chief.

I asked Cathy how she managed taking care of the family and crew during a busy race day. She smiled while looking at the organized scramble of activity going on in front of us as several teams made last-minute adjustments during the final practice of the day. "I'm used to the chaos. What would life be without chaos?" Cathy said with a smile.

According to Cathy, her signature dish would be her pot roast. "I cook it on the grill and the guys love it!" But if there was a down side to traveling the race circuit and being away from their Chicago home, it would be not being able to get her hands on her favorite, secret ingredient. "I use this one kind of dressing. It's called western dressing. You can't find it anywhere except near home. So every chance I get, I stock up."

CATHY'S TIPS FOR TAILGATING: Always make sure to have something for the crew to nibble on. We do a taco salad or Mexican dip that they can snack on all day. Keeps them happy!

Rockingham Hot Rub Seasoning

This rub comes from some fans in Rockingham, North Carolina.

½ cup cayenne pepper
½ cup salt
½ cup chili powder
¼ cup paprika
1 tablespoon black pepper
1 tablespoon garlic powder
1 tablespoon cumin powder
1 tablespoon brown sugar

Combine ingredients well, and store in a shaker.

Steak Rub

2 tablespoons black pepper
2 tablespoons salt
1 tablespoon celery powder
1 tablespoon Italian seasoning

Combine all of the ingredients and rub over steaks a few hours before grilling.

Submitted by Jeff – Kentucky – Dale, Sr. and Dale, Jr. fan

Jim Stevenson of Smithfield Meats heads up the grilling and smoking crew for the Frank Kimmel - National Pork Board / Advanced Auto Parts team. Jim estimates that during the lunch break at this one race, he will serve 1700 smoked pork sandwiches to hungry crews in the ARCA garage area.

Tex-Mex Seasoning

Looking for a south-of-the-border flavor to spice up your next meal? This blend of spices makes a great seasoning, or you can even use it as a simple taco seasoning for browned ground beef.

¼ cup minced onion
¼ cup minced green bell pepper
¼ cup chili powder
2 tablespoons garlic powder
2 tablespoons cumin powder
½ tablespoon salt
½ tablespoon pepper

Combine ingredients well and store in refrigerator until ready to use.

Note: You can substitute hotter peppers for the bell peppers, if desired.

Jim's Jack and Double Cola Steak Marinade

I met Jim outside the Huntsville Speedway during an O'Reilly's Southern All Star Series (SAS) race.

⅓ cup Jack Daniel's
⅔ cup Double Cola
¼ cup steak sauce
1 tablespoon minced garlic
1 tablespoon lemon juice
Large dash of salt
Large dash of pepper

Combine all ingredients and use as a marinade for steak.

Submitted by Jim L. Anderson – South Carolina
Lowes Motor Speedway fan

Chef Tom's Marinade

4 cups orange juice
1 cup soy sauce
2 tablespoons chopped garlic
½ cup Dijon mustard
½ cup honey
1 teaspoon cayenne pepper

Whisk all ingredients together until well blended.

Submitted by the National Pork Board
www.otherwhitemeat.com

Top Fuel Barbecue Marinade Sauce

This is a perfect recipe for a sauce or a marinade for those race fans who like it HOT.

½ cup ketchup
½ cup Dijon mustard
⅓ cup hot pepper sauce
2 tablespoons Worcestershire
2 tablespoons steak sauce
1 tablespoon meat tenderizer
1 tablespoon minced onion
2 tablespoons minced garlic
1 tablespoon jalapeño juice

Combine everything in a saucepan and simmer. Allow the sauce to cool, then marinate your meat in it overnight, or use as a baste.

Submitted by Robert C. – NHRA fan

Stacy Compton rolls the #59 Kingsford Ford into position for a qualifying run.

HITTING THE PITS

Nothing makes a great main dish better than a great side dish. Side dishes come in many shapes and sizes at the track. Baked beans, veggies, soups, salads and more are all on the menu. The great thing about side dishes is that there are so many versions. I have tried a GA-ZILLION versions of coleslaw and baked beans! But almost every one of them is different; each one has its own flavor. Here are several tailgate side dishes you can whip up at the track or in the comfort of your own kitchen before you head out. Have fun!

- **Salads**
- **Vegetables**
- **Pasta and Rice**
- **Sandwiches**
- **Chilies**

SALADS

Tailgate Macaroni Salad

4 cups elbow pasta, cooked and drained
3 stalks celery, finely chopped
1 cucumber, chopped large
⅓ cup bacon bits
⅔ cup mayonnaise
2 tablespoons milk
1 tablespoon parsley
1 teaspoon onion powder
1 teaspoon celery seed
Salt and pepper to taste

Mix all of the ingredients together in a big bowl. Refrigerate until ready to serve.

Submitted by Jason and Carla – Georgia – NASCAR campers and fans

Easy Pasta Salad

This is possibly the easiest pasta salad ever.

1 package favorite pasta
1 bag frozen veggies
Bottled Italian salad dressing
⅓ cup sliced or chopped almonds

Cook the pasta and drain well. Allow frozen veggies to thaw; pat dry. Stir together all ingredients, chill, if possible, and serve.

Submitted by Sarah B. – Atlanta, GA – Ricky Rudd fan

Tech Racing Ranch and Bacon Pasta Salad

1 box ranch and bacon-flavored pasta salad
½ cup mayonnaise
1 cucumber, chopped
1 tomato, chopped
½ pound bacon, cooked and crumbled

Empty pasta mix into 3-quart (or larger) saucepan ⅔ full of boiling water. Gently boil uncovered for 15 minutes, stirring occasionally. Drain; rinse with cold water. Shake well to drain. In a large bowl, stir together seasoning mix and ½ cup mayonnaise. Stir in pasta salad, chopped cucumber, tomato and bacon.

Submitted by Tim and Tammy Chambers – Tech Racing team owners

Jake Says —

For easy salads, buy those pre-cut bags of lettuce and mixed salad greens. Each bag makes about four or more bowls. No fix time and no cleanup.

Ham and Pasta Salad

3 cups uncooked rotini
1 cup cubed ham
1 cup shredded Cheddar cheese
½ cup cubed bell pepper
½ cup cubed red bell pepper
1 tablespoon vegetable oil
1 tablespoon olive oil
¼ cup lemon juice
1 teaspoon garlic salt
1 teaspoon dried dill weed
Salt and pepper to taste

Cook rotini; drain and rinse. Place in a large bowl and gently mix with remaining ingredients; cover and chill. Serve cold with a dash of Parmesan cheese.

Mark Martin is one of the top-five NASCAR drivers on the Nextel Cup circuit and perhaps one of the best stock car drivers ever. In addition to his superior driving ability, Mark is one of the finest individuals you would ever want to meet. To many in the garage area, Mark is the complete race driver . . . one of the best who's ever lived. He can build the cars, fix them and drive them with style, class and a code of conduct that demands respect.

Shrimp Pasta Salad

1 bag pasta shells, cooked
1 small box cooked, frozen mini shrimp
1 bottle Italian dressing
¼ cup minced green pepper
¼ cup diced onion
¼ cup diced squash
¼ cup grated Parmesan cheese
1 squirt of lemon juice

Combine all ingredients, stir and chill before serving.

Submitted by Carol – Lowe's Motor Speedway tailgater

Tom's Potato Salad

Tom says, "My mom always made this potato salad for picnics and family cookouts. When I started camping at racetracks, I learned how to make it."

1½ cups mayonnaise
3 tablespoons cold milk
2 tablespoons apple cider vinegar
1½ tablespoons prepared mustard
2 tablespoons sugar
2 teaspoons celery seed
Bacon bits
Salt and pepper to taste
Freshly ground black pepper
8 cups cooked potato chunks
1 bunch scallions, sliced
3 tablespoons minced chives
6 hard-cooked eggs, chopped
Parsley

Mix everything in a large bowl and toss gently to coat all of the potato pieces. According to Tom, this recipe is best if made early and allowed to sit in the fridge, covered, for several hours, or even overnight.

Submitted by Tom A. – Racetrack camper

Mandy's "Tater" Salad

According to my buddy Mandy, this is the best tater salad you'll ever put in your mouth. Mandy and her husband are huge Bristol race fans.

1 dozen or so medium-size potatoes
1 medium onion, chopped
2 teaspoons celery seed
½ jar sweet pickle relish
2–3 boiled eggs
1–1½ cups mayo
1 tablespoon mustard

Boil potatoes with skins until tender. (I usually boil them in a huge kettle for about an hour.) Cool completely. Peel and cube. Add onion, celery seed and pickle relish; mix. Refrigerate overnight.

Next day, or before serving, add boiled eggs, mayo and mustard and mix well.

Submitted by Mandy Picket – Athens, TN – Rusty Wallace fan

Terry's Creamy Potato Salad

5 pounds red potatoes
1 cup light mayonnaise
1 cup Miracle Whip Salad Dressing
¼ cup skim milk
2 tablespoons mustard
Salt and pepper
½ green onion, finely chopped
1 bunch radishes, diced
1 teaspoon minced garlic
4 hard-cooked eggs, crumbled
¼ cup chopped almonds

Dice and boil potatoes until tender. Mix mayonnaise, Miracle Whip, milk and mustard until smooth. Add additional milk, if needed. Add salt and pepper to taste. Gently stir in potatoes, green onions and radishes; blend well. Before serving, stir in eggs and almonds. Chill and serve cold.

Submitted by Terry McDaniels – NASCAR / Dale Jr. Fan

Tom Buzze

Driver – ARCA / USAR Hooters Pro Cup
#16 Naturally Fresh Ford Taurus

When I first met Tom, he was knee-deep in kids showing them his car at a media event outside of Atlanta before a race the next day. I stood back and watched this young man as he greeted families and kids of all ages with a smile.

"I started racing with go-karts and open-wheel modifieds." Not only does Tom bring a youthful enthusiasm to the track, he also brings a lot of mechanical knowledge. In fact, he built his own open-wheel modified in 2002 and won 7 races, 6 in a row.

I asked Tom the big difference between his open-wheel race car and his Naturally Fresh Ford Taurus. "Size and weight! The big difference I first noticed was how these big cars handle in the turns." According to Tom, his eye-opening experience came the first time he practiced in a stock car. "I hit the gas and went into my first turn after I got up to speed and thought to myself . . . man, these things don't stop!"

ACHIEVEMENTS: Fort Pierce Kart Championship 1997, Tri-County Championship 2002, Tri-County Championship 2003, Winning streak of 6 wins.

FAVORITE FOOD: When I hit the grill, I'm a traditional cheeseburger type of guy. You can also toss in a nice salad with PLENTY of Naturally Fresh dressing.

Andy's Easy Coleslaw

Andy was in college a few years back when he decided to make some coleslaw in the middle of the night. "I remembered how my grandmother used to make it and it was real simple. Sometimes in college you just have cravings. Mine was coleslaw." Now when Andy and his buddies tailgate, he is in charge of coleslaw.

½ cup sugar
⅓ cup apple cider vinegar
⅓ cup Italian dressing
1 small green or red bell pepper, finely chopped
2 pounds finely shredded cabbage
2 medium-size carrots, finely chopped
Salt and pepper to taste

Mix well, cover and chill before serving.

Submitted by Andy – South Boston, VA – Michael Waltrip's biggest fan

Crunchy Coleslaw

A neat version of coleslaw that pops up at many tailgate parties.

2 packages chicken-flavored ramen noodles
¾ cup seasoned rice wine vinegar
6 tablespoons oil
3 tablespoons sugar
1 teaspoon freshly ground black pepper
½ teaspoon salt
2 spice packs from the noodles
1 large head green cabbage, shredded
¼ head red cabbage, shredded
3 carrots, shredded
5 scallions, sliced
1 cup sliced toasted almonds

Open the ramen noodles and finely crush them in a bowl; set aside. In a larger bowl, combine vinegar, oil, sugar, pepper, salt and spice packets. Stir in cabbage, carrots, scallions and almonds. Wait until right before you serve the coleslaw to add the crushed noodles (for a better crunch).

Note: If you want the noodles soft, add them when you make the coleslaw.

Camping Coleslaw

Sandra says this coleslaw needs to be made before you head to the track. "An extra day really makes it taste good!"

1 small head cabbage, finely shredded
1 small head red cabbage, finely shredded
4 carrots, finely shredded
1 bunch scallions, sliced
1 cup mayonnaise
¾ cup buttermilk
⅓ cup sugar (or to taste)
2 tablespoons lemon juice
2 tablespoons white wine vinegar
1 teaspoon salt
1 stalk celery, minced
1 teaspoon paprika
Large dashes of salt and pepper

Combine everything and toss well. Put in a sealed container and chill overnight.

Submitted by Sandra – Martinsville, VA – NASCAR fan and camper

Deck Chef Tip!

Coleslaw and Camping

Any foods like slaw, potato salad, deviled eggs, etc., should be kept in chilled, airtight containers if made before coming to the track. In fact, you should have separate cold storage for items like this—away from ice used in keeping beverages cold.

Marinated Slaw

MARINADE:

1 pint cider vinegar
2½ cups sugar
1 teaspoon salt
1 teaspoon mustard seed
1½ teaspoons celery seed
½ teaspoon turmeric

Heat the above ingredients to just boiling; cool.

1 head cabbage
2 onions
1 (4-ounce) jar chopped pimentos

Chop, shred or grind (food processor) the cabbage and onion. Pour Marinade over the cabbage and onion. Stir in the pimentos. Refrigerate for 24 hours. This will keep for up to 3 weeks in the refrigerator.

Submitted by Tony Taffar – Gasman/Cook
#16 Naturally Fresh USAR Hooters Pro Cup Series

Casey Atwood waits to get into his car before green flag racing gets underway for a NASCAR BUSCH Series race.

VEGETABLES

Marinated Cucumbers

¾ cup sugar
2 teaspoons salt
¼ cup white vinegar
1 quart sliced cukes
1 medium onion, thinly sliced
½ bell pepper, thinly sliced

Stir sugar, salt and vinegar together until dissolved. Pour over vegetables. Refrigerate overnight.

Submitted by Tony Taffar – Gasman/Cook
#16 Naturally Fresh USAR Hooters Pro Cup Series

The Best Way to Cook Corn, Ever

This is a GREAT recipe for RACE DAY!

Get as many fresh ears of corn as you need (preferably a sweet corn). Gently pull back the husks of the corn from top to bottom, making sure not to rip them off. Remove silks. Tie a string around the husks to form a handle at the bottom of the corn which you will use to turn the corn when you place it on the grill. Brush melted butter on the corn and place on the grill over low coals. You can cook them around the edges of your kettle or gas grill and they will not burn. Turn frequently and brush on lots of butter. Grill around 15 minutes or until tender. To kick it up a notch and add a nice smoky flavor, you can also add chopped chipotle chiles to the butter. Happy grilling!

Submitted by Skip "The GrillMaster" Van Dette, and
Susan "The GrillMaster's 'Sue Chef'" Van Dette
Chattanooga, TN – Jeff Gordan / Dale, Jr. fans

Carol's Tailgate Corn

2 (15-ounce) cans whole-kernel corn, drained
1 red bell pepper, diced
1 green bell pepper, diced
1 small onion, diced
2 tablespoons butter
Dash of garlic powder
Salt and pepper to taste

Combine all ingredients in a skillet, and cook until corn becomes tender. More butter can be added as needed.

Submitted by Carol – Lowe's Motor Speedway tailgater

Boiled Beer Corn

8 ears whole corn on the cob
2 (12-ounce) cans beer
Sugar, salt and pepper to taste

Combine everything in a large pot. Add enough water to help cover. Boil until done; serve hot.

Submitted by the Davies – Concord, NC – Tailgating family

Kris's Grilled Carrots

Another one of Kris' health-conscience recipes.

1 bag whole carrots
Olive oil
Italian seasoning

Clean and cut the carrots lengthwise. Brush with a light coat of olive oil. Grill till the way you like them. Sprinkle with Italian seasoning and serve.

Submitted by Kris P. – Photographer – Race fan

French Fried Carrots

½ pound carrots
½ cup flour
1 teaspoon sugar
1 teaspoon salt
1 egg
3 tablespoons milk
Bread crumbs
Oil for frying

Scrape carrots; cut in 2-inch lengths. Combine flour, sugar, salt, egg and milk. Dip carrots in batter; roll in bread crumbs and deep-fry in hot oil.

Janet's Foil Pack Dinner

When Janet Guthrie, NASCAR driver, cooked for her crew, she often would make a full veggie meal cooked in a foil packet.

2 zucchini, sliced
2 red bell peppers, sliced
1 green bell pepper, sliced
½ onion, sliced
2 tablespoons olive oil
Your favorite herb or seasoning

Baste all of the veggies with the olive oil, adding a bit more oil, if needed. Coat with your favorite herb or seasoning. Divide into manageable portions, wrap in foil and cook over hot coals.

Submitted by Janet Guthrie – NASCAR Driver

HEY RACE FANS, did you know that Casey Atwood became the youngest pole winner in NASCAR BUSCH Series history when he grabbed the pole at just 17 years old?

Mushroom Soup Green Beans

Here is a simple green bean casserole that you can cook on the grill.

2 (16-ounce) cans French-cut green beans
1 (10¾-ounce) can cream of mushroom soup
1 beef bouillon cube
Salt and pepper to taste
1 (3-ounce) can French fried onions

In a large saucepan, cook green beans and cream of mushroom soup with the bouillon cube. Add salt and pepper. When done, serve in a bowl and top with onions.

Submitted by B. L. – Houston, TX – Texas Motor Speedway fan

Carla's Franks and Baked Beans

2 (28-ounce) cans baked beans
½ cup brown sugar
½ cup ketchup
⅓ cup mustard
¼ cup steak sauce
¼ cup hot sauce
Large dashes of salt and pepper
1 small onion, chopped
1 package hot dogs, sliced thin
1 hot pepper (Anaheim pepper is best)
3–4 strips bacon, uncooked, cut into small pieces

Combine everything and cook in a baking dish or in a crockpot until heated through.

Submitted by Jason and Carla – Georgia – NASCAR campers and fans

New England Baked Beans

This recipe is simply divine. They do take a long time to cook, but are easy and inexpensive.

½ pound bacon, cooked, divided
3 (16-ounce) cans pork and beans
4 tablespoons molasses, or 6 tablespoons light molasses
1 teaspoon mustard
1 teaspoon grape jelly
Salt to taste

Put half of the bacon in the bottom of bean pot and add beans; mix molasses and other seasonings with a little hot water and pour over the beans. Place the remaining bacon on top, cover the pot and cook in a slow oven (250°) for 3–4 hours. Keep the lid on the bean pot until the last hour of cooking, then uncover, and allow the beans and bacon on the top to brown.

The Dalton Gang

Hixson Motorsports
www.hixsonmotorsports.com

Talk about some of the best fans in the world! Hixson Motorsports of Soddy Daisy, Tennessee, may very well have them. Eric Hays is a race fan and has been in the grocery business for several years. "I met Ron Cox and Wayne Hixson during a fundraiser. I realized I could help them like they were helping me by bringing show cars to fundraisers I helped out with. I asked if there was anything I could do to help the team. Cooking some meals was what we agreed on."

After a few grill sessions for the team, Eric is now the official "garage chef" for Hixson Motorsports. According to Fiona Shaffer, PR director for Hixson Motorsports, Eric and his crew of friends are now known as the "Dalton Gang," named after Dalton, Georgia, where most of them are from.

"We come to as many races as we can, and provide some hot meals, snacks and such. When I can't get to a race, I will pack up the meals to send with them." In appreciation for the efforts of Eric, his wife Jennifer and the rest of the gang, the Hixson Motorsports team paid them the ultimate compliment. "When Jennifer and I were married, they put 'Congrats Jennifer and Eric 9/13/03' across the back bumper of the car. "It was the least we could do," Fiona said with a smile.

ERIC'S BARBECUE TIPS: "I use about forty pounds of pork, slow smoked for about twelve hours, then hand-pull it. To keep it moist for race day, I blend in just enough sauce to keep it fresh. That way I can keep it moist, heat it up and get two meals."

Black Baked Beans

A great twist on a baked bean recipe.

2 (16-ounce) cans pork and beans
2 (16-ounce) cans black beans, rinsed and drained
½ cup taco sauce
1 package taco seasoning
1 (4-ounce) can green chilies
1 tablespoon chopped cilantro
Lime juice

Combine all, and cook in a foil pan until beans thicken. You can cook in an oven or right on the grill. Use some foil to lightly cover the pan. Serve hot.

Jill's Broccoli and Cheese Casserole

1 small onion, chopped
1 stick butter or margarine
1 (10¾-ounce) can cream of celery soup
1 (8-ounce) jar Cheez Whiz
1 cup rice, cooked
3 stalks broccoli, steamed, or 1 (20-ounce) bag frozen broccoli, thawed
1 can Durkee dried onions

Simmer onion in margarine; add soup, Cheez Whiz, rice and broccoli. Put in baking dish, top with Durkee dried onions and bake at 350° for 45–60 minutes, until broccoli is done. Serve as a side dish or a meal.

Note: Use reduced-fat margarine, soup and Cheez Whiz for lower calories, with just as much taste.

Submitted by Jill Lezotte – ARCA pole board creator

Big Show Baked Vegetables

- 4 tablespoons olive oil, divided
- 1 red bell pepper, sliced into thin strips
- 1 green bell pepper, sliced into thin strips
- 1 yellow onion, sliced into thin strips
- 1 zucchini, thinly sliced
- 1 small eggplant, thinly sliced
- 1 large tomato, thinly sliced into half circles
- 2 cloves garlic, minced
- ¼ teaspoon oregano
- ¼ teaspoon basil
- Salt and pepper to taste
- ¼ cup John Boy and Billy's Grillin' Sauce

Coat the bottom of a 9-inch pie pan with 2 tablespoons olive oil. Alternate the vegetables in layers, seasoning as you go with garlic, oregano, basil, salt and pepper, until the pan is full. Combine the remaining olive oil with the John Boy and Billy's Grillin' Sauce, and drizzle over the vegetables. Cover with foil and bake in a 400° oven for 40 minutes.

Used with permission of Big Tom Price
www.bigshowfoods.com

Kent "The Deck Chef" Whitaker (right) and Big Tom Price of bigshowfoods.com (home of John Boy and Billy's Grillin' Sauce) settle down for a race after a day of feeding hungry race fans.

Campfire Grilled Veggies

Kris is a big race fan. "I hit a track wherever I go. I camp 2–3 times a year." After a bout with cancer and some other health issues, Kris says he cooks mostly veggies, fish and chicken these days. "Simple stuff with good taste is what I am looking for."

1 yellow squash, sliced
1 zucchini, sliced
1 onion, sliced
1 green bell pepper, sliced
6 red potatoes
Fresh mushrooms, cut in half
Salt, pepper and any spices you like to taste
Butter

Combine everything and split evenly into foil packs. Grill over medium heat. Serve hot.

Submitted by Kris P. – Photographer – Race fan

Marinated Mixed Veggies

1½ cups red wine vinegar
¾ cup olive oil
¼ cup sugar
1 tablespoon Cajun seasoning
1 tablespoon hot sauce
1 tablespoon minced garlic
1 sweet onion, sliced
2 large red bell peppers, chopped
2 large green bell peppers, chopped
2 (15-ounce) cans green beans, drained
1 head cauliflower, broken up
1 bunch broccoli, broken up
1 cup fresh mushrooms, sliced
1½ cups cherry tomatoes

In a medium saucepan, combine first 6 ingredients, and bring to a boil. Remove from heat and cool. In a medium saucepan over medium-high heat, blanch onion, peppers and green beans for one minute. Combine all vegetables in large, non-aluminum bowl. Pour in marinade and mix until vegetables are thoroughly coated; cover. Allow to chill in refrigerator for several hours.

Submitted by Sheri "The Chef" and Foster – BUSCH Series fans

Veggie Munch

Ask Linda what an easy recipe is for her next tailgate and she will say "adding ice to a drink!" Then she will give you this very simple recipe for a zingy twist to some fresh veggies.

1 pound broccoli, cut into small pieces
1 red bell pepper, cut into small pieces
1 yellow bell pepper, cut into small pieces
1 small onion, cut into pieces
2 carrots, cut into small pieces

Get the idea? Next, put all of the veggies into a large zip-close bag and add the following:

1½ tablespoons olive oil
1½ tablespoons soy sauce
Large dash of Cajun seasoning
Large dash of garlic powder

Shake the bag real good and store until needed. Wrap in foil at your tailgate and toss on the grill, in the foil, for 10–15 minutes. "I like mine to still have some crispness, but if you cook them longer, they almost steam in the foil."

Submitted by Linda W. – Dover International Raceway tailgater

Deck Chef Tip!

Soup it up!

Frozen veggies are fine for any tailgate. They are easy to store and quick to prepare. Combine a large bag of assorted mixed veggies with a few cans of your favorite soup in a large saucepan and have a great side to any race-track meal.

Big Bad Baked Vidalia Onions

4 jumbo Vidalia onions
1 cup lightly salted butter, softened
1/4 cup brown sugar
1 teaspoon rosemary
1 teaspoon thyme
4 cloves garlic, finely chopped
12 tablespoons John Boy and Billy's Grillin' Sauce

Cut off the bottom of each onion. Cut the skin off each onion in 1/4-inch-wide strips, from the bottom wide end to the narrow top end, leaving the skin connected at the top. Mix the butter, brown sugar, rosemary, thyme and garlic together. Divide and place equal amounts on the center of 4 separate sheets of heavy-duty aluminum foil. Place an onion, flat (cut) side down, onto each piece of the foil, over the butter mixture. Pull up the strips of onion skin and raise the corners of the foil. When the sides are high enough, add 3 tablespoons John Boy and Billy's Grillin' Sauce to each. Hold the skin strips straight up and crimp the foil around the neck of the onion, leaving the skin on the outside. Place the onions on a cookie sheet, and bake at 375° until tender (or cook on the grill).

Used with permission of Big Tom Price
www.bigshowfoods.com

HEY RACE FANS, did you know that in 1991, Terry Labonte won the first NASCAR BUSCH Grand National race at Watkins Glen? This began an impressive streak of four wins in six years, including three consecutive wins in '94 through '96.

Grilled Mexican Potatoes

4 large potatoes
Olive oil
1 package chili seasoning

Cut potatoes into 8 lengthwise sections, or smaller if needed. Brush with olive oil and sprinkle with chili seasoning. Cook over medium heat on grill, using foil, if needed. Brush with olive oil and add more chili seasoning as you cook. Serve hot with sour cream and a big juicy steak!

Make-Ahead Mashed Potatoes

When I was working on my first cookbook, Smoke in the Mountains, *I did a profile on Sweetwater Valley Farm. Somewhere during the interview, racing came up. This recipe was given to me by one of the employees of Sweetwater Valley Farms, and she said it is perfect for tailgates and race-day parties.*

10–12 medium potatoes, cooked
2 cups whole milk, heated
1 stick butter, melted
½ cup sour cream
1 tablespoon salt
½ teaspoon pepper
½ cup (or more) Sweetwater Valley Farm Cheddar cheese

Mash potatoes, then add remaining ingredients except the cheese. Spoon into a buttered 9x13x2-inch baking dish. Cover tightly and keep refrigerated up to 2 days. To reheat, simply place covered dish into a 350° oven and cook about 20 minutes. Remove foil, top with cheese and continue heating until cheese melts, about 10 minutes.

Submitted by Sweetwater Valley Farm – Sweetwater, TN

Parmesan Cheese Potatoes

6 potatoes, sliced
½ cup butter
1 tablespoon grated onion
Salt and pepper to taste
Large dash of paprika
Italian seasoning
Grated Parmesan cheese

Grill, bake, or fry potatoes while basting with butter. Sprinkle with onion, seasonings and cheese after removing from heat. Serve hot.

Submitted by Sheri "The Chef" and Foster – BUSCH Series fans

Even though the gas can and the car are now fitted with safety devices to limit the amount of fuel spills, the gas can remains about the same as it has for years. The long handle and neck design allow the gasman to pick up the can, vault the wall, start to fill the car and perform the rest of his duties as gravity pulls the gas from the can into the car.

PASTA AND RICE

Pesto Chicken and Pasta

It's not often you find a dish like this at a tailgate. But when you do, it's a pleasure to sink your teeth into it. Anthony asks, "Do you always have to have steaks and burgers?"

1 pound boneless chicken, cooked
Olive oil
Garlic powder
½ cup plus 2 tablespoons freshly grated Parmesan cheese, divided
2 (16-ounce) packages pasta shells, cooked
1 (16-ounce) container prepared pesto
1 teaspoon Italian seasoning
1 (10-ounce) box frozen chopped spinach, thawed, drained
2 tablespoons lemon juice
1½ cups mayonnaise
½ cup milk
1 cup cashew halves and pieces
1 (16-ounce) package frozen tiny baby peas

Brown the chicken in the olive oil, garlic powder and 2 tablespoons Parmesan cheese. Cube into bite-size pieces. Cook, then drain the pasta. Blend the pesto, Italian seasoning, spinach and lemon juice in a blender. In a bowl, combine the pesto mixture, mayonnaise, milk, cashews, frozen peas and cooked chicken, and mix well. Combine with pasta and remaining ½ cup cheese. Serve this as a chilled salad or with the hot chicken spooned over the pasta.

Submitted by Anthony C. – Tony Stewart fan

Meaty Mac and Cheese

This is a meaty version of mac and cheese that makes for one heck of a side or a hot main dish. I ate this under a tarp at a track in the Carolina's during a rainy weekend of racing.

2 cups elbow macaroni, cooked and drained
1 small onion, diced
1 small red bell pepper, diced
½ pound ground sausage, browned
½ pound ground beef, browned
2 cups shredded Cheddar cheese
1 cup shredded Monterey Jack cheese
½ cup milk
Salt and pepper to taste
Garlic powder
Additional cheese for topping

Combine everything except cheese for topping. Bake at 350° in a coated dish for about 30 minutes or until thickened. Top with cheese, and bake until cheese melts. Serve hot.

Submitted by K. Brooks – South Carolina
Dirt track junkie / NASCAR fan

Jake Says—

Precook ground beef at home. Drain the excess fat and store frozen in zip-close freezer bags, then just open a premeasured bag as you need it.

Tim Fedewa

Driver – NASCAR BUSCH
#12 NBS 24/7 Chevrolet

Tim proudly shares the limelight before a race with one of his biggest fans from St. Jude Children's Research Hospital. Tim is an outstanding cook who specializes in Italian dishes.

I was introduced to Tim Fedewa by Fitz / Bradshaw rep, David Walker and NASCAR BUSCH Series manager of communications, Rick Houston. "I know a driver you have to meet," Rick said with a gleam in his eyes. Later that day at the track, David called and said, "Meet us in the pits. We have about ten cars in front of us before we practice."
I waited as Tim signed a few autographs. He reached over to shake my hand and I told him he was about to get questions he had never been asked at the track. "Try me," Tim said.

When I asked about his love for cooking and knowledge on Italian cuisine, Tim's eyes lit up. "I love cooking!" According to Tim, and members of his crew, Italian food is one of his favorites. "I try to watch what I eat. I like healthy foods. Mostly before a race, I will load up on carbs and Italian. I'll eat that for about two days before a race."

But being at the track does mean a few other foods sneak in the pre-race diet. "Every once in a while I will do a big hot dog. Come on, it is a racetrack!" Tim said with a smile.

NEAT THINGS: *NBS 24/7* stands for NASCAR BUSCH Series 24 hours a day, 7 days a week, the television show. Armando Fitz and Hall of Fame NFL Quarterback Terry Bradshaw co-own Tim's car.

Camp-Out Mac and Cheese

You can do this recipe in a pot over a fire, or in a baking dish in the oven. It's great for tents, RVs or kitchens.

1½ cups elbow macaroni
Salted boiling water
½ stick butter
2 tablespoons all-purpose flour
Large dash of salt and pepper
2 cups cubed Velveeta cheese
Grated Parmesan cheese

In a pot, boil the noodles and drain; stir in remaining ingredients except Parmesan, and simmer over low heat until thick. If cooking in an oven, place in a dish and bake about 30 minutes at 350°. Top with grated Parmesan cheese and serve.

Submitted by K. Brooks – South Carolina
Dirt track junkie / NASCAR fan

Longtime ARCA RE/MAX Driver Ron Cox waits in his car for the green flag to drop during a qualifiying run. Ron told me the day was great until the sun came out. "We had to wait and wait for other cars. Things were going slow, but then SUN! Man, it gets hot quick in these cars!" Ron has teamed with a Tennessee high school to teach classes on the motorsports industry.

Mushroom Beef and Noodles

This is perhaps the easiest recipe I have ever made for beef tips and noodles.

1 pound cheap beef steaks
Salt and pepper to taste
Steak sauce or soy sauce
1 (10¾-ounce) can cream of mushroom soup
1 package quick-cooking seasoned noodles (ramen)
Water as needed for the noodles

Grill steaks, and dash with salt and pepper. Brush with steak sauce or soy sauce. When done, slice into small pieces and continue to cook over low heat, basting occasionally with half the mushroom soup. Meanwhile, cook noodles as directed on package. When noodles are just about done, stir in remaining soup. Top with steak strips and serve hot.

Submitted by Tim – Frank Kimmel / ARCA RE/MAX fan

Deck Chef Tip!

No dogs, please!

Prepared chicken nuggets or even breaded tenders, dipped in sauce and placed over the grill on a skewer, are easy to prepare for kids wanting something other than a hot dog.

Chicken Bog

1 whole chicken
1 pound breakfast sausage links
Salt and pepper to taste
1 onion, chopped
1 bell pepper, chopped
1 (10 3/4-ounce) can cream of mushroom soup, undiluted
1 pound rice

Boil chicken until done. Remove from broth and reserve broth. Pick meat from bones, and cut into pieces. Cook sausage in a frying pan and cut into 1-inch pieces. Salt and pepper broth to taste. Bring to a boil. Add chicken, onion, pepper, sausage and soup. Reduce the heat to simmer; cover and cook for 30 minutes or longer, if desired.

Thirty minutes before serving, return the broth to a boil. Add rice and reduce the heat to low. Cook until the rice is done, adding more water if necessary. Remove from heat; cover and let stand for 10 minutes. Serve with crackers and Texas Pete sauce.

Submitted by Tony Taffar – Gasman/Cook
#16 Naturally Fresh USAR Hooters Pro Cup Series

Carla's Veggies and Rice

1 1/2 cups rice
1/2 stick butter plus 2 tablespoons butter, divided
3 1/2 cups water, divided
1/2 tablespoon minced garlic
1 red bell pepper, diced
1 zucchini, sliced
1 onion, finely diced
6 mushrooms, sliced
1 beef bouillon cube
1 teaspoon Tabasco sauce

Bring rice, 1/2 stick butter and 2 1/2 cups water to a boil, then reduce heat and simmer. In a skillet, sauté minced garlic, red pepper, zucchini, onion and mushrooms in remaining 2 tablespoons butter. Add remaining 1 cup water, bouillon cube and hot sauce. Simmer to reduce water. Serve over rice.

Submitted by Jason and Carla – Georgia – NASCAR campers and fans

Aleah's Bacon Fried Rice

This recipe is very filling and can be used as a main dish or as a side dish.

1 pound bacon cooked, drained and crumbled
3 cups water
2 cups rice
1 teaspoon olive oil
3 tablespoons butter
1 medium onion, chopped
3 eggs
1 tablespoon soy sauce
½ teaspoon adobo seasoning

Bring water to a boil; add rice and olive oil. Reduce heat to low, cover and cook for about 20 minutes. In a large skillet, melt butter, stir in onion and cook until golden. Move onion to the edge of the skillet and scramble eggs. Stir in soy sauce and adobo seasoning. When eggs are just about done, add in rice and bacon. Stir to mix, and serve hot.

Aleah's fried rice tip: If you want to make this more of a main dish, you can add in additional ingredients such as peas, chives or whatever you would like to add more color.

Submitted by Aleah Russell – Dale Earnhart, Jr. fan

The media frenzy is on! Camera's click away as Cup drivers approach their cars to the claps and cheers of fans in the stands just moments before racing.

SANDWICHES

Egg Salad Sandwich

6 hard-boiled eggs shelled and crumbled
2 celery stalks, minced
½ onion, finely chopped
½ cup mayonnaise
1 teaspoon Parmesan cheese
¼ teaspoon salt
Dash of pepper
Dash of garlic powder

Combine all of the ingredients. Do not overmix—if you do, your egg salad will be too mushy. Spread on your favorite bread with lettuce and tomato.

Submitted by Marie and Charles – NASCAR campers

Crunchy Cucumber Sandwiches

1 (8-ounce) package cream cheese, softened
2 tablespoons mayonnaise
2 tablespoons sour cream
2 tablespoons minced onion
1 teaspoon minced garlic
½ teaspoon Worcestershire sauce
Large dash of salt and pepper
2 cucumbers, minced
⅓ cup chopped almonds
1 teaspoon parsley
Mini deli bread slices, or white bread, halved

Combine all ingredients except bread. Serve on small deli slices of party bread, or halved or quartered loaf bread. It is also great with crackers.

Submitted by Marie and Charles – NASCAR campers

On the Grill Grilled Cheese Pita Sandwich

Grilled pita sandwiches, or just plain pita sandwiches, are a very popular sandwich along the racing circuit. Why? They are easy and quick.

1 pack pita bread, cut in half and opened
Assorted favorite cheese slices
Olive oil

Open the pita bread and stuff with your favorite cheeses. Lightly brush the outside of the bread with olive oil. Cook on the grill until cheese melts. Serve hot.

Chicken Pita Sandwich

1 envelope vegetable soup mix
1 cup sour cream
2 (11-ounce) cans chicken
1 small onion, chopped
½ green bell pepper, chopped
½ cup bacon bits
Pita bread, halved

Combine everything except bread in a bowl. Spoon into pita bread halves or on regular bread.

Deck Chef Tip!

Say cheese!

What makes a great sandwich for many is often the cheese. You can up the flavor of any sandwich with assorted cheeses instead of just American and processed cheese slices. This is a great way to make some fantastic grilled cheese sandwiches.

Baked Spam and Cheese Pita Sandwiches

1 block American cheese, shredded
3 hard-boiled eggs, crumbled
1 can Spam, diced
2 tablespoons chopped onion
2 tablespoons chopped green olives
2 tablespoons sweet relish
4 ounces cream cheese, softened
Pita bread halves

Mix all of the ingredients together and spoon evenly into halved pita bread. Wrap in foil, and grill until insides are hot.

Submitted by Marie and Charles – NASCAR campers

Jim's Racing Gyros

Jim suggests making the meat in advance and storing cold or frozen in a zip-lock bag.

1 pound ground beef
2 tablespoons water
1 tablespoon lemon or lime juice
1 teaspoon salt
½ teaspoon ground cumin
½ teaspoon oregano
¼ teaspoon pepper
½ tablespoon minced garlic
1 small onion, chopped
2 tablespoons olive oil
4 pita breads, cut in half
½ cup plain yogurt
1 teaspoon sugar
1 small cucumber, finely chopped
1 medium tomato, finely chopped and towel dried
2 cups shredded lettuce

In a skillet, brown ground beef, then drain. Add water, lemon juice, salt, cumin, oregano, pepper, garlic, onion and olive oil. In a bowl, mix remaining ingredients well. Spoon equal amounts of meat and lettuce mixture into opened pita halves.

Submitted by Jim A. – Nashville Superspeedway camper

Cajun Chicken Wraps

If you are looking for something filling during a tailgate, try one of these wraps. You can premake as much as you feel you need. Heck, precut your lettuce, dice your 'maters and onions and just spend the time at the track heating up some chicken.

2 pounds chicken breast or tenderloins
1 small onion, minced
½ stick butter
¼ cup beer
Hot sauce
Cajun seasoning
Garlic powder
Salt and pepper to taste
Lettuce, tomato, onion, green pepper

Clean and dry chicken. In a large skillet, brown chicken with the onion, butter, beer and hot sauce. As chicken cooks, begin to cube or shred it. When done, cover with Cajun seasoning, garlic powder, salt and pepper as desired. Serve hot in a wrap topped with your favorite veggies and maybe a splash more hot sauce!

Chicken Salad Wraps

Sometimes you just have to have a good wrap!

3 cups cooked cubed chicken
¼ cup diced red onion
¼ cup diced sweet onion
½ cup chopped walnuts or almonds
½ tablespoon minced garlic
½ teaspoon salt
½ teaspoon pepper
¼ cup mustard
4 cups mayonnaise (or less)

Combine all of the ingredients, cover and chill. Serve wrapped or on old-fashioned bread or croissants.

Submitted by Marie and Charles – NASCAR campers

Tracey Chambers

Driver – Stock, Late Model, Weekly
www.techracing.com

Growing up in a racing family, where her father was a former go-kart winner and was an active Late Model crew chief, Tracey attended most races at the Orange County Speedway as a little girl. It was only natural for Tracey to decide she wanted to race, too.

After spending the winter helping to build a pure stock, four-cylinder race car, Tracey strapped into the driver's seat at the age of seventeen. She brought the car home in third that night and was hooked.

Tracey decided she was ready for the next step, so she decided to make the jump to the Modified Four-Cylinder Division in 2000. Tracey collected four top-fives and eleven top-tens out of fifteen starts. She earned co-rookie of the year honors as well as being tied for fifth in the points rankings. She also racked up seven pole positions and two wins, becoming the first female to win at Orange County Speedway in Rougemont, North Carolina. She cracked into the top-five ten times and never finished outside the top six. She narrowly missed capturing her first championship by a mere four points after leading them for over half of the season.

In addition to her success in the driver's seat, Tracey was personally invited by Funkmaster Flex to participate in the Funkmaster Flex Super Series Invitational. She was also extended an invitation to attend the prestigious Lyn St. James Driver Development Program to be held at Phoenix International Raceway. When not racing, Tracey serves as a crewmember and spotter for her brother's late model stock team and attends college classes.

Chicken Taco Wraps

3 cans chunk chicken pieces
2 tablespoos olive oil
1 tablespoon seasoned salt
1 tablespoon chili powder
½ tablespoon cumin
3 or 4 limes, cut in quarters
Pinch of garlic powder
Tortillas or veggie wraps

Mix the chicken with oil, seasoned salt, chili powder and cumin. Place in a zip-close bag or covered container and allow to marinate. Cook chicken in a well-oiled skillet or griddle on the grill using medium heat. While the chicken is cooking squeeze with lime and sprinkle some garlic powder on top for extra flavor. Serve in a wrap with your favorite taco toppings.

Steak Fajita Wrap

2 pounds flank steak
½ cup chopped onion
¼ cup chopped cilantro
½ tablespoon ground cumin powder
½ cup lime juice
Jalapeño peppers, sliced
Sliced onion
Sliced green pepper

Slice steak into thin strips. Combine everything into a skillet and cook until steak is done.

Flour tortillas
Cheese
Lettuce
Guacamole

Wrap steak strips in soft-shell tortillas with cheese, lettuce and guacamole.

Mike's Creole Sandwich

2 loaves Italian round bread
Spicy Creole mustard (Dijon, if you are a sissy)
Hot sauce
½ pound sliced salami
½ pound sliced ham
½ pound hot pepper cheese
½ pound provolone cheese
½ pound mozzarella cheese
2 cans chopped olives
2 (4-ounce) cans diced green chiles
2 carrots, minced
2 stalks celery, minced
Olive oil

Open the bread, and top with some mustard and hot sauce. Add meats and cheeses. In a bowl, combine remaining items to make an olive oil paste. Add more or less olive oil as needed. Spoon on top of each pile of meat and cheese. Close sandwich; serve hot or cold.

Submitted by Mike L. – Racing / LSU fan

Before any race, a car must go through inspection. Here inspectors measure the car with templates to make sure it fits series specs. They also look for other rule, equipment, set and safety violations. If a car fails, it must go back to the garage for a fix—hopefully before the inspection area closes. Don't worry, many cars are inspected after the race as well to make sure no "adjustments" were made.

Speedway Muffulettas

TOPPING:

Chopped olives
Pickled peppers
Carrots
Celery
Olive oil

Mix Topping items, and grind them in a blender for a few seconds.

SANDWICH:

Round bread
Salami
Ham
Pepper cheese
Provolone cheese
Mozzarella cheese
Mustard
Cajun seasoning
Lemon juice

Make your Sandwich with all of the meats, cheeses, seasoning and lemon juice. Spread Topping over the meat and buns. Wrap in foil, and grill about 4–5 minutes each side.

Submitted by Rebecca and Charles – NASCAR fans and campers

Grilled Reuben Sandwiches

Rye bread
½ stick butter, softened
⅓ pound deli-sliced corned beef
8 ounces sauerkraut, drained
⅓ cup Thousand Island dressing
Swiss cheese
Salt and pepper to taste

Butter both sides of bread slices and brown one side of each in a skillet. On the toasted side of the bread, add corned beef, sauerkraut, dressing, Swiss cheese, salt and pepper. Add another piece of bread, toasted side down, and grill on both sides with butter until cheese melts.

Jim A. – Nashville Superspeedway camper

Grilled BLT and Cheese

Perfect for a late breakfast or late lunch.

Cooked bacon
Lettuce
Sliced tomato
Texas toast
American cheese slices
Swiss cheese slices

Make a regular bacon, lettuce and tomato sandwich on Texas toast, then add a few slices of cheese. Butter the outsides and grill to make a great BLT.

Submitted by Russ – NASCAR / BUSCH fan

Ray's Frozen Chicken Cordon Bleu Sandwich

Ray has the right idea. Good food can be frozen and cooked quick at the track.

1 package frozen chicken patties, breaded or unbreaded
Sliced ham
Sliced Swiss cheese
Mayo
Dijon mustard
Hamburger buns
Lettuce
Tomato

Cook chicken per package directions. "We deep-fry 'em." Top with ham, cheese and a mixture of mayo and mustard. Serve on a bun with lettuce and tomato.

Submitted by Ray and his crew – Talladega / Daytona race fans

Tony Taffer, gasman and chef, does his job at a Hooters Pro Cup race in Concord, North Carolina.

Tailgate Turkey Sausage

This recipe is great for those looking to cut a bit of fat from their diet. However, you can use regular sausage if you prefer.

48 turkey sausages
6 large sweet onions, sliced
4 green peppers, sliced
3 red peppers, sliced
1 teaspoon minced garlic
Paprika
Crushed red pepper
Ketchup and hot sauce

Boil sausages in water. While cooking, add the sliced veggies and garlic. Cook until veggies are almost done. Place sausage and veggies on the grill using heavy foil or a grill griddle cover. Cook until sausages begin to brown. Add paprika, red pepper and a bit of ketchup and hot sauce. Mix well and serve hot on a bun.

Hot Honey Mustard Turkey Loaf Sandwiches

This is a race-day recipe that I tried at a dirt track somewhere in North Carolina. It was a way a mom could serve her family something hot off the grill besides a hot dog.

1 frozen turkey loaf
1 bottle honey mustard
1 pack large dinner rolls or buns
Your favorite cheese

Allow turkey loaf to thaw in the fridge before heading to the track. Keep on ice or in cooler until needed. Slice the loaf in ¼-inch or larger slices as evenly as possible. Hold the loaf together slightly and cover with honey mustard. Get in between each slice. Wrap in foil and place on covered grill using medium-high direct heat. Cook about 15 minutes for all four sides. Cook to an internal temp of 165°. Serve on toasted dinner rolls with your favorite cheese.

Homestead Cuban Sandwich

Carlo says, "This is a recipe for a Cuban sandwich that I grew up with. You can make it with no cleanup, heat it on the grill, wrap it in foil, and bake it or just eat it cold. You can use French bread instead of Cuban bread."

1 loaf Cuban or French bread
½ cup squeeze mustard
1 tablespoon hot sauce
Salt and pepper to taste
Dash of garlic
½ pound thin-sliced Swiss cheese
½ pound thin-sliced deli ham
½ pound thin-sliced roast beef or roast pork
Thin-sliced dill pickles

Slice the bread lengthwise and open. Combine mustard, hot sauce, salt, pepper and garlic; spread over both pieces of bread, using all of the spread mix. Layer cheese on the bottom and top pieces of bread. Put meat in the middle and then pickles. Cover with the top piece of bread and cheese. Makes 6 medium-size sandwiches or 4 big ones.

Submitted by R. Sims, Sr. and family
Florida race fans / Homestead tailgaters

Tires are the lifeblood of race teams. In addition to great driving, skilled crew members, gas rationing and set-up, tires are VERY critical. Teams are issued tires for the race. Different series and tracks determine if you get four changes or more.

Baked Beef and Cheese Sandwich

A great sandwich that is very easy to make and can be doctored up to your own taste.

Individual loaves of French bread
Your favorite cheese slices
Thin-sliced roast beef
Sliced onions
Sliced green peppers
Minced garlic
Steak sauce
Soy sauce

Open the loaves of bread and add slices of cheese. Combine remaining ingredients, and cook until onions become tender. Do not overcook. Add more steak sauce or soy sauce to keep meat moist. Do not drain. Put equal amounts on each bun. Wrap in foil and place over low heat on your grill. Serve hot.

Submitted by Russ – NASCAR / BUSCH fan

Grilled Philly Cheese Steak Sandwich

4 pounds sandwich steak (flank or round)
2 onions, sliced
2 green peppers, sliced
Olive oil
Steak sauce
Minced garlic
French rolls
American cheese
Mozzarella cheese

Pound the steak into thin pieces. Grill over medium heat with foil underneath. Add onions and peppers. Baste with olive oil, steak sauce and minced garlic, and continue to cook until done. Divide onto French rolls. Top with cheeses. Wrap each sandwich in foil, and keep warm until served.

Scott Rice

Weekly Driver
#33 Birmingham International

"Sometimes the rain gets ya!" With a smile, Scott Rice was holding out his hand catching rain drops as they fell from the sky. "Seems like I have been rained out more this season than I have raced!" Scott was loading his two cars after action at the speedway was canceled due to heavy rains and lightning.

"I have two cars, one for dirt and one for asphalt. I have been in this for several years. My dad used to race so I knew I wanted to do it, too." According to Scott, racing in weekly series at three or four tracks a year around the state is a hard job that he could not do alone. "I could not do this without my family and friends. We build everything and fix everything. It's all done by us."

But all of the hard work does pay off. "The most fun time I have ever had racing was winning the mid-season championship. Plus, it doesn't matter what track you go to, you see your buddies and such. It's fun." According to Scott, he has been racing since the mid-90s and plans to keep racing.

SCOTT'S FAVORITE TAILGATE FOOD: "If I was home watching the Daytona 500 with my friends and grilling out, I would have to fix up some big ole steaks and some chops!"

Quick Philadelphia Cheese Steak Sandwich

1 thinly sliced rib-eye or eye roll steak
1 large onion, sliced
green and red bell peppers, sliced
6 tablespoons oil
4 crusty Italian rolls
Canned Parmesan cheeseSweet

Cook the steak and slice into thin pieces. Sauté veggies in oil. Place on a bun and top with cheese. Serve hot.

Submitted by Russ – NASCAR / BUSCH fan

Tailgate Tenderloin Sandwich

2 pork tenderloins, about 1 pound each
Chef Tom's Marinade (page 143)
8 kaiser rolls, sliced in half
Orange Aïoli Sauce (page 134)
2 tomatoes, thinly sliced
3 cups chopped loose-leaf lettuce
1 Vidalia onion (or any sweet onion), thinly sliced

Place pork tenderloins in 2 heavy-duty, resealable bags. Pour half of Chef Tom's Marinade in each bag and seal; marinate in refrigerator for 8–24 hours.

Prepare medium-hot grill. Remove pork from marinade; discard marinade. Grill pork 15–20 minutes, or until internal temperature is 160°. Toast rolls on the grill. Spread Orange Aïoli Sauce on toasted side of rolls. Slice tenderloins for sandwiches, and layer pork onto bottom of rolls; add tomatoes, lettuce and onion.

Texas Toast Steak Sandwich

Grab some Texas toast, and some cheap steaks for a good sandwich.

4 cheap steaks
Meat marinade
Cheese
Butter
Texas toast

Slice steaks thinly with a knife, but do not shred or cut all the way through. Marinate as long as possible. Grill until done. Top with cheese. Place between 2 pieces of buttered Texas toast, and cook like a grilled cheese sandwich.

Pan-Grilled Country Ribs Open-Face Sandwich

Only takes three ingredients and people at your tailgate will think you are a grilling master.

A few pounds country ribs
1 bottle barbecue sauce
1 package Texas toast

Place the ribs and sauce in a large foil pan. Cover with foil and place on the grill. Let the ribs cook and simmer in the sauce for a few hours. Remove from heat and serve the tender meat over some Texas toast. You could serve with slaw, onions and a bit of hot sauce, if desired.

Honey Pork Chop Sandwich

4 boneless pork loin chops, at least ½ inch thick
1½ cups apple juice
¼ cup soy sauce
2 tablespoons honey
1 clove garlic, minced
Salt and pepper to taste
4 deli buns

Marinate chops in remaining ingredients except buns and grill. Baste with remaining sauce as you cook. Serve on a bun with your favorite toppings.

Submitted by Dan B. – Georgia

Mike's Meatball Sandwich

A big pot of these makes for great snacks during the race. Mike says, "Just place some toothpicks next to them so people won't use their fingers."

1 pound ground beef
½ pound ground breakfast sausage
⅔ cup fine cracker crumbs
½ cup evaporated milk
½ cup minced onion
¼ cup minced pepper (hot or bell)
½ tablespoon black pepper
½ tablespoon garlic powder
½ tablespoon oregano
1 teaspoon salt
1 egg
1 cup barbecue sauce

Mix all together except barbecue sauce. Form into balls and bake in 350° oven until done (20–30 minutes, depending on size). Place in a bowl and toss with barbecue sauce. Serve on a deli hot dog bun with cheese or just with toothpicks!

Submitted by Big Mike – Alabama – Jr. Johnson fan

Deck Chef Tip!

Mama Mia!

If you don't have time to make your own meatballs, buy a bag of frozen meatballs, then dress them up with some special sauce at the track.

Grilled Ham Steak Pockets

4 ham steaks, cut in half
Butter
Brown sugar
Peppers
Onions
Cheese
Hot sauce
1 (8-count) can crescent rolls

Brown ham steaks in butter and brown sugar. When done, grill veggies in butter and remaining juice. Cut ham into small enough slices to fit inside a flattened crescent roll. Add cheese, grilled veggies and hot sauce, if desired. Fold crescent roll over enough to cover. Bake or place in a covered grill until golden brown.

Texas Toast Grilled Ham and Cheese

A HUGE grilled cheese sandwich that makes for a great meal. You can add just about any cheese you want, but this has three of my favorites.

Texas toast
Butter
Honey
White American cheese slices
Mild Cheddar slices
Jalapeño cheese slices
Ham slices

Combine 2 parts butter with 1 part honey. Spread over one side of the Texas toast. Layer your cheeses, add some ham and cook in a hot skillet until golden brown. You can also skip the butter part until the last and cook these babies on the grill. Flip once and spread some honey butter over the grilled sandwich before serving.

HEY RACE FANS, did you know that the BUSCH Series was named in 1984 when Anheuser Busch, Inc. of St. Louis, Missouri, became the sponsor of the NASCAR Budweiser Late Model Sportsman Series?

2-Foot-Long Fish Stick Sandwich

This is a HUGE version of a po' boy!

1 bag frozen fish sticks
Cajun seasoning
Lemon juice
1 loaf deli-style French bread
1/4 head lettuce, chopped
Jalapeño peppers, sliced
Tomatoes, very thinly sliced
Creamy coleslaw
Tartar sauce
Hot sauce

Deep-fry or bake the fish sticks. As soon as they are done, sprinkle with Cajun seasoning and a bit of lemon juice. Open the loaf of bread and add fish sticks, lettuce, peppers, tomatoes and coleslaw. Mix the tartar sauce with some hot sauce and serve on the side.

Submitted by Russ – NASCAR / BUSCH fan

Easy BBQ Shrimp Sandwich

1 cup butter, melted
1/3 cup extra virgin olive oil
2/3 cup ketchup
1/4 cup Worcestershire sauce
1/4 cup brown sugar
Salt and black pepper to taste
1 lemon, juiced
1/4 cup hot pepper sauce
1/4 cup Italian seasoning
1 tablespoon minced garlic
1 teaspoon paprika
4 pounds jumbo or medium shrimp, peeled and deveined

In a large covered pan, combine all of the ingredients except the shrimp, and bring to a simmer over medium heat. Add shrimp, and cook until shrimp begin to turn pink. Remove from sauce and place on the grill to finish cooking. Baste with remaining sauce. Serve hot on a warm French roll.

CHILIES

Speedway Canned Chili Supreme

2 (16-ounce) cans chili with beans
2 (16-ounce) cans chili without beans
1 (16-ounce) can hot chili beans
1 (10-ounce) can diced tomato and green chiles
2 (4-ounce) cans green chiles
1 small onion, diced
1 cup water
1 package chili seasoning
1 tablespoon garlic powder
Hot sauce as desired

Combine everything in a large pot and simmer on low about 2 hours. Serve hot over brats, dogs or corn chips, and make sure to add some sour cream.

Submitted by Daniel – NASCAR nut

Corn Chili

1 pound ground beef
1 pound ground hot pork sausage
2 tablespoons minced garlic
1 package chili seasoning
1 (14.5-ounce)can stewed tomatoes
1 (12-ounce) can beer
2 (16-ounce) cans whole-kernel corn
2 (16-ounce) cans kidney beans
1 large onion, chopped
1 tablespoon cumin powder
1 green bell pepper, chopped

Brown meat, then drain. Combine all ingredients in a large pot, and cook over medium heat for 2 or more hours. Serve hot.

Veggie Chili

Here is a very simple chili recipe for veggie lovers.

2 (16-ounce) cans kidney beans
1 (16-ounce) can Northern beans
1 (16-ounce) can pinto beans
1 (16-ounce) can black beans
1 (16-ounce) can black-eyed peas
1 (14½-ounce) can diced tomatoes
1 (8-ounce) can tomato sauce
1 large onion, chopped
1 green bell pepper, chopped
1 (15-ounce) can vegetable broth
2 packages chili seasoning
1 teaspoon cumin powder
Salt, pepper and hot sauce to taste

Combine everything in a large pot, and simmer for several hours. According to Thomas, this chili is great served with hot corn bread, or even French bread instead of crackers.

Submitted by Thomas and Cynthia A. – Stock car and dirt track fans

Deck Chef Tip!

Breaking it down

The secret to great veggie chili is the use of assorted beans for taste and texture. Avoid overstirring so that your spoon does not break down the beans. This could cause your veggie chili to look like a modified bean dip! BUT, any remaining veggie chili could be broken up with a fork or food processor for a great dip!

Super Bean Chili

Use dry beans if possible and soak them overnight. "But if you're in a pinch, just open up some cans!"

½ pound kidney beans
½ pound white Northern beans
¼ pound black beans
¼ pound pinto beans
¼ pound navy beans
5 pounds ground beef
5 large onions, chopped
¾ cup minced garlic
2 packages chili seasoning
¼ cup paprika
¼ cup cayenne pepper
¼ cup crushed red peppers
3 (14½-ounce) cans stewed tomato
2 (8-ounce) cans tomato sauce
Hot sauce (optional)

Soak the beans together overnight in water. Drain water and add fresh water to cover. Cook on medium heat about 2 hours. Brown meat, drain grease and add meat to beans. Add remaining ingredients, and hot sauce, if desired. Cook covered for several hours.

Submitted by Barton – BUSCH Series fan

Carolyn's Chili

2 pounds ground beef
1 tablespoon olive oil
¼ cup Tabasco sauce
1 medium onion, chopped
2 (16-ounce) cans kidney beans
4 tablespoons chili powder
2 (14½-ounce) cans tomatoes
1 cup water
2 tablespoons salt
2 tablespoons pepper
2 tablespoons sugar
2 tablespoons Worcestershire sauce
2 tablespoons cumin powder
2 tablespoons oregano

Brown ground beef in oil; drain fat. Combine remaining ingredients with beef, and simmer covered for several hours.

Submitted by Carolyn – Kasey Kahne / Jeff Gordon fan

Texas Motor Speedway Chili

This recipe comes from Wanda and her husband Frank. They love the races at Texas Motor Speedway and this is their standard pot of chili. "We do REAL chili here in Texas!"

2 pounds lean chuck roast
1 (1-pound) package bacon
2 onions, minced
1 green bell pepper, minced
1 red bell pepper, minced
½ cup chopped jalapeño peppers
1 tablespoon cumin powder
2 (14½-ounce) can diced tomatoes
2 tablespoons minced garlic
2 teaspoons salt
5 tablespoons chili powder
1 tablespoon oregano

In a large pot, brown meat and bacon with onions and peppers. Drain excess fat. Crumble bacon and cut the beef into small pieces. Combine all ingredients, and cook on medium for about 3 hours.

Submitted by Wanda and Frank – Texas – Race fans

Many young drivers get their start in racing on smaller tracks along the smaller racing series. O'Reilly Auto Parts Southern All Star Series is a great learning place for young drivers as well as a competitive series for seasoned pros.

Fajita Steak Chili

3 pounds cheap strip steaks
4 tablespoons cumin powder, divided
¼ cup olive oil
2 pounds smoked sausage, finely diced
2 (14½-ounce) cans diced tomatoes
2 large cans hot chili beans
2 (10-ounce) cans beef broth
½ cup chili powder
1 package taco or fajita seasoning
⅓ cup sliced jalapeños
2 (8-ounce) cans tomato sauce
4 large onions, chopped
⅓ cup hot sauce
2 teaspoons paprika
1 tablespoon crushed red pepper
¼ cup red wine vinegar
1 (12-ounce) can beer

Rub steak with 2 tablespoons cumin powder. Slice into bite-sized pieces. In a large skillet, brown the sliced steak in olive oil. Add sausage, and brown. Add more oil, if needed. In a large pot, all ingredients, including meat mixture. Cover and stir every once in a while as needed. According to John, he cooks huge amounts of this chili using his gas-fired turkey fryer. "I put it behind something to block wind, turn it on low and cook for as long as possible."

Submitted by John and Belinda H. – NASCAR campers and race fans

Linda's Cinnamon Chili

1½ pounds ground beef
1 onion, chopped
2 cloves garlic, minced
2 (16-ounce) cans light red kidney beans, rinsed and drained
1 (24-ounce) jar Chi-Chi's Mild Chunky Salsa
2 teaspoons chili powder
½ teaspoon oregano
½ teaspoon cumin
Dash of cinnamon (up to ¼ teaspoon)

Brown ground beef, onion and garlic. Drain. Add beans, salsa and spices; mix well. Simmer 1 hour to blend flavors.

Submitted by Linda Renninger – Dover International Speedway

Brandon Miller

Driver – NASCAR BUSCH
#21 Reese's Racing
www.brandonmillerracing.com

Macee Whitaker with NASCAR BUSCH #21 Reese's Driver, Brandon Miller

Heading into Nashville, Brandon Miller had some big shoes and big finishes to fill. In 2003 Johnny Sauter nearly won as the Reese's driver. In 2004, after a final lap wreck, driver Clint Boyer thrilled fans with a fourth place finish for the team.

"I'm excited about this weekend, I really like the track and it's nice that I have seen it before." Brandon had seen the track before because while climbing the ladder of racing success, he filled in as a back-up driver for Robby Gordon. He practiced and qualified the car for Gordon in 2004.

Being a fan favorite, the driver of the Reese's car is always sought by fans for a few autographs. "I like your car and your suit," one young fan told Miller as he walked slowly to pit row signing autographs along the way. Brandon made sure this young fan had an autograph.

Brandon is one of the upcoming young and exciting drivers in NASCAR. Brandon drives along with Kevin Harvick the #21 Reese's Car for Richard Childress Racing (www.rcrracing.com) located in Charlotte North Carolina. Born in California, Brandon makes his home in Huntersville, North Carolina.

Jo's Basic Chili

2 pounds lean ground beef
3 cloves garlic, minced
3 tablespoons chili powder
1 large red onion, chopped
3 banana peppers, chopped
3 japapeño peppers, chopped
2 large cans stewed tomatoes
2 cans hot chili beans
1 can Campbell's beef broth
½ tablespoon cumin powder
2 teaspoons garlic powder

Brown beef; mix everything together in a slow cooker and let it go! Jo says she sometimes adds some crushed bacon as well.

Submitted by Jo – West Virginia – Bristol / Any short track fan

Racing, Rescue, Venison Fire House Chili

This is a recipe from a buddy who is a huge race fan, as well as a hunter and a fireman. He loves going to the races and other tailgates. "When we head up to Bristol, we always make a big pot of chili on the first night." This makes a TON of chili, so it feeds a huge crowd!

2 pounds boneless sirloin
2 pounds boneless venison roast
2 pounds ground beef
2 pounds hot ground breakfast sausage
Olive oil
½ cup sliced jalapeño peppers with juice
1 (12-ounce) can beer
1 cup bourbon
1 (12-ounce) can cola
⅓ cup hot sauce
3 large onions, chopped
2–3 bell peppers, chopped
3 (8-ounce) cans tomato sauce
4 tablespoons minced garlic
½ cup chili powder
1 tablespoon crushed red pepper
2 tablespoons cumin powder

Brown meat in oil. Cube the sirloin and the venison into small pieces. Make sure the ground beef and the sausage are broken up well. Drain all excess grease. In a large pot, combine all ingredients and cook over low to medium heat for many hours. Keep covered, and add more beer or water if it gets too thick.

Submitted by – T. C. – North Georgia – Rusty Wallace fan

Cajun Boiled Chili

1 pound ground beef
1 pound smoked sausage, sliced thin
1 pound crawfish meat
1 pound mini shrimp
3 (16-ounce) cans hot chili beans
1 (8-ounce) can tomato sauce
1 large onion, chopped
4 tablespoons chili powder
⅓ cup hot sauce
2 tablespoons minced garlic
2 teaspoons salt
2 teaspoons pepper
2 tablespoons Cajun seasoning
1 tablespoon hot sauce
1 cup water
½ cup white wine (optional)

Brown beef and sausage. Break beef into small pieces. Combine all ingredients, and cook for several hours. This recipe is great with chips, bread, crackers and even rice.

Jake Says—

Make a chopped dawg plate by topping a sliced-up smoked sausage or footlong dog with chili, cheese, onions, hot sauce and slaw!

Chopped Steak Chili

4 pounds chopped sirloin
½ cup olive oil
1 stick butter
2 (8-ounce) cans tomato sauce
2 (16-ounce) cans chili beans
1 (12-ounce) can beer
3 medium onions, chopped
1 large red bell pepper, chopped
5 tablespoons chili powder
2 tablespoons minced garlic
1 tablespoon oregano
1 tablespoon cumin powder

Brown steak in olive oil and butter. Do not drain. Combine all ingredients in a large pot, and simmer covered for several hours, adding water, as needed.

Submitted by Harold and Brenda – North Carolina

Campfire Chicken Chili

2 pounds cooked, cubed chicken
4 cups water
1 package chili seasoning
2 (16-ounce) cans Northern beans
1 (15-ounce) can chicken stock
1 stick butter
2 chopped celery stalks
⅓ cup sliced jalapeño peppers
1 teaspoon dill seeds
1 teaspoon crushed white peppercorns
1 large onion, chopped fine
1 tablespoon minced garlic
1 tablespoon chopped fresh basil
1 block mozzarella cheese, grated

Add the chicken to remaining ingredients in a pot; cover. Cook at a low temperature, loosely covered to allow some of the moisture to cook off. Cook as long as possible.

Submitted by Harry and Jess – Tennessee – NHRA / AMA fans

MIS White Chili

1½ pounds boneless skinless chicken breasts
3 (16-ounce) cans white northern beans
1 block colby Jack cheese, grated
1 (16-ounce or larger) jar salsa

Clean, bake and cube the chicken. Combine all ingredients in a crockpot, and cook on LOW for a few hours. Serve hot with tortilla chips.

Note: I added a bit of water and some chili powder to my version of this chili. It makes a GREAT topping for tortillas!

Submitted by Michigan International Speedway
Chickie Miller – MIS Operations Assistant

Chicken Chili

1–2 tablespoons olive oil
2 green bell peppers, chopped
1 banana pepper, chopped
2 onions, chopped
3 celery stalks, chopped
1 tablespoon minced garlic
4 (16-ounce) cans white Northern beans
2 (10-ounce) cans diced tomatoes with juice
2 pounds diced cooked chicken
1 (16-ounce) can whole-kernel corn
1 (15-ounce) can chicken broth
1 package chili seasoning
1 (10¾-ounce) can cream of chicken soup
1 teaspoon black pepper
1 cup grated Cheddar cheese for topping

Combine all ingredients except cheese. Cook over medium heat until thick. Serve hot. Top with cheese.

Submitted by Daniel R. – Race fan

Cajun Crawfish Chili

Pete says he was not born a Cajun but somehow it got into his blood. This is a great recipe that you can do with or without the crawfish.

1 pound ground beef
2 pounds cooked crawfish
2 (16-ounce) cans hot chili beans
½ cup Cajun seasoning
1 onion, minced
1 bell pepper, minced
1 tablespoon garlic powder
2 teaspoon salt
1 teaspoon pepper
2 tablespoons soy sauce
2 tablespoons hot sauce
1 tablespoon dried parsley
4 tablespoons chili powder
1 (8-ounce) can tomato sauce

Brown meat; combine all ingredients and cook until you feel like eating it! Add water or beer as needed.

Submitted by Pete L. – Camper / Indy and Brickyard fan

Race officials quickly begin to surround the top ten cars after a race as they head to the post-race inspection area. The cars in many series are checked before and after each race to make sure they are within the rules.

Chili Dog Casserole

Simple version of Chili Dog Casserole that kids (and adults) are sure to love.

3 boxes Jiffy Corn Bread Mix
1 cup grated Cheddar cheese, divided
1 package hot dogs
2 (16-ounce) cans chili

Mix all of the corn bread mix together according to package directions. Grease a baking dish or foil pan. Place half of the corn bread mixture along the bottom. Gently spread some cheese across. Slice and dice the hot dogs into small pieces. Top cheese layer with hot dogs, then chili. Cover with remaining cheese and then remaining corn bread mixture. Bake at 325° about 20 minutes or until corn bread turns golden brown.

Chili Corn Bread Casserole

2 (16-ounce) cans chili with beans
2 boxes Jiffy Corn Bread Mix
1 small onion, diced
1 cup shredded Cheddar cheese
Milk as directed on box

Combine all ingredients in a large bowl, then spoon into a greased cake pan. Bake at 350° about 20 minutes, then turn. Cook until corn bread turns golden brown.

TOPPING:

1 cup shredded Cheddar cheese
¼ cup minced onion
1 tablespoon chili powder
1 tablespoon hot sauce

Mix Topping ingredients and evenly spoon over the top of the dish. Put back in oven until cheese melts. Serve hot with a spoon!

Submitted by Laurie – Wife of a crazy NASCAR fan (said with love and a smile)

Bev's Chili Biscuits

2 cans large biscuits
1 cup crushed corn chips
1 or 2 (16-ounce)cans chili with beans and meat
Favorite shredded cheese

Open the canned biscuits and place them in greased or nonstick muffin pans. Gently spread the biscuit to form the muffin shape. Gently press a light coating of corn chip crumbs into the sides of the biscuit. Fill with a spoonful or so of chili. Bake in the oven until edges of biscuits turn brown. Top with cheese, and serve hot. Bev said she started this recipe using puff pastry, but the biscuits made it more "tailgate-y," and super easy.

Kent's Corn Bread Twist on Bev's Chili Biscuits:
I made a thick corn bread mix and placed a spoonful of this into a nonstick muffin pan. In the center, I placed a small spoonful of chili that had been mixed with some grated cheese and a few extra spices. I topped this with another bit of corn bread mix to cover the chili. I baked it at 350° degrees until the corn bread was a deep golden brown. It took a bit of trying to find the right amount of chili to use in the middle. If you use too much, the corn bread muffin will break apart when you take it out of the pan.

Submitted by Bev – Tennessee – Huge Jimmy Spencer and Ward Burton fan / Wife of a nutty Jeff Gordon fan

THE FINAL LAP

The infield of any racetrack is a great place to get a good meal, as are the campgrounds and parking lot tailgate parties. But we all know that the sweet tooth takes over every once in a while. The recipes in this section vary from ones that may take some skill to recipes that combine boxed snack cakes and creativity. So here are a few great desserts bound to take the checkered flag for any tailgate meal. Or if your are like me . . . you may start with these dishes before you ever make it to the main dish. Nothing wrong with that!

COOKIES AND BROWNIES

MIS No-Bake Cookies

1½ cups butter
1¼ cups peanut butter
½ cup cocoa
½ cup milk
4 cups sugar
2 teaspoons vanilla
½ teaspoon salt
5½ cups oats

Melt the butter, peanut butter and cocoa over low heat in a large pot. Add milk and mix well. Stir in sugar to dissolve; leave pot on low heat. Stirring occasionally, bring to a rolling boil, then remove from heat. Add vanilla, salt and part of the oats. Coat well, then add remaining oats a little at a time. Mix well at a good speed. Immediately scoop onto parchment-lined sheet tray and let cool.

Submitted by Tim Olszewski – American Honda Hospitality Chef
Michigan International Speedway
Used with permission of MIS

Pit crews are watching and waiting during a long green flag stretch of racing.

Cinnamon Refrigerator Cookies

2¼ cups flour
½ cup granulated sugar
1 cup butter or margarine (2 sticks)
1 egg, separated
3 tablespoons brown sugar, packed, mixed with 1 teaspoon cinnamon (or more to taste)

Preheat oven to 350°. In mixing bowl, combine flour and sugar. With fork, cut butter till particles are pea-sized. Add egg yolk, and mix dough with hands till smooth. Divide in half, and shape into 2 logs about 1½ inches in diameter. Brush logs lightly with beaten egg white, then roll in cinnamon and brown sugar mixture. Chill at least 1 hour (maybe longer).

Cut ½-inch slices. Bake on greased cookie sheet for 12–15 minutes or until golden brown. Makes about 60 cookies.

Submitted by Debbie and Greg Stewart
South Bend, Indiana – Andy Belmont racing

40-Year-Old Brown Sugar Drops

"I've been baking these cookies for forty years. They are a favorite with my family."

1 cup soft shortening
2 cups brown sugar
2 eggs
½ cup sour milk or buttermilk
1 teaspoon baking soda
1 teaspoon salt
½ cup chopped nuts (optional)

Thoroughly mix shortening, brown sugar and eggs. Stir in sour milk or buttermilk. Sift together and stir in baking soda and salt. Stir in nuts, if desired. Bake 8–10 minutes at 400°. Chill at least 1 hour.

Drop rounded teaspoonfuls about 2 inches apart on lightly greased baking sheet. Bake until set, just until almost no imprint remains when touched lightly with finger. Don't overbake.

Note: To make sour milk, add 1 tablespoon vinegar or lemon juice to 1 cup of milk.

Submitted by Norma Cooksey – Mother of Joe Cooksey, driver of the #23 Hixson Motorsports / 1-800 Serve-Pro ARCA RE/MAX car

Cheddar Cheese Cookies

WHAT? Cheese cookies? Yep, I tried this recipe for a race-day event and people loved them.

1 cup sugar
1¼ cups powdered sugar
1½ sticks butter
1 cup oil
2 eggs
1 teaspoon vanilla
¼ cup whole milk
4½ cups all-purpose flour
1 teaspoon baking soda
1 teaspoon cream of tartar
½ teaspoon salt
1½ cups quick oats
1 cup grated Sweetwater Valley Farm Cheddar cheese
1 cup chopped pecans

Cream sugars, butter and oil. Add eggs, vanilla and milk. Mix well. Mix dry ingredients, adding gradually to first mixture. Stir in oats, cheese and pecans; chill and drop by teaspoon onto cookie sheet. Bake at 350° for 10–12 minutes or until golden brown.

Submitted by Sweetwater Valley Farm – Sweetwater, TN

Simple Chess Snacks

1 (18¼-ounce) box yellow cake mix
4 eggs, beaten, divided
1 stick butter, melted
1 (8-ounce) bar cream cheese, softened
1 (1-pound) box powdered sugar

Mix cake mix, 1 beaten egg and butter together. Spread evenly into a greased and floured pan. Mix cream cheese, powdered sugar and remaining 3 beaten eggs. Mix well and pour over cake mix. Bake at 350° about 30 minutes or until browned. Allow to cool some before serving and cutting.

Submitted by Holly J. – Concord, NC – Race fan

Marc Mitchell

Driver – ARCA RE/MAX Series
#34 University of Alabama Chevrolet

Professional driver Marc Mitchell has roared on to the racing scene and is giving his career the "old college try" with help from Auburn University, sponsor of the #34 Chevrolet. "I'm having a real fun time! The university has been great."

The 21-year-old Auburn student already has some success behind the wheel, picking up Late Model Rookie of the Year honors at Senoia Speedway in Georgia, as well as the 2001 Legends Cars rookie award. This year, Mitchell ran a limited schedule on the ASA National Tour. Next season, look for Mitchell as he debuts on the NASCAR BUSCH Series at select races.

When I asked about favorite foods, grilled foods and pit foods, Marc drew a blank except for one thing. "Well, I guess I'm pretty much a traditional guy when it comes to grilling and such. But the only food NOT allowed in my garage or pit area is peanuts!" According to Marc, he was told that the peanuts he was eating were bad luck on a race day. Shortly after that, he wrecked his car! "That was all it took for me!" the young man said as a smile grew across his face.

Hot Fudge Cookie S'Mores

Lisa says this is more of a "method" than a recipe. You can use any style of cracker, cookie, topping, marshmallow or whatever you like. This just happens to be one of her favorites.

1 package large sugar cookies
1 jar marshmallow crème
1 bottle fudge topping, warmed

Place a sugar cookie in a bowl or on a plate. Spoon a layer of marshmallow crème onto the cookie; top with warm fudge and another cookie.

Submitted by David and Lisa – Rusty Wallace / Michael Waltrip fans

Jake Says —

Having an assortment of store-bought snack cakes around is always a good idea for a race weekend.

No-Bake Peanut Butter and Chocolate Bars

1 (6-ounce) bag chocolate chips
2 tablespoons butter
3 tablespoons peanut butter
5 cups crispy rice cereal
¼ cup crushed peanuts

Slowly melt chocolate chips, butter and peanut butter. Stir in cereal and nuts. Pour into a 9x13-inch cake pan lined with wax paper. Allow to cool. Remove from pan and cut into equal pieces.

Submitted by David and Lisa – Rusty Wallace / Michael Waltrip fans

Congo Bars

Butter and flour for preparing baking pan
2¼ cups flour
2 teaspoons baking powder
⅛ teaspoon salt
½ cup (1 stick) plus 2 tablespoons unsalted butter, cut into chunks
1 (16-ounce) box light brown sugar
3 large eggs
12 ounces good-quality semisweet chocolate chips (see note)

Arrange an oven rack at the center position and preheat the oven to 350°. Generously butter a 9x13-inch baking pan, then dust it with flour. Shake out any excess flour.

Sift together the flour, baking powder and salt; set aside. Melt butter in a large, heavy saucepan over medium heat. Remove from heat and stir in brown sugar until dissolved and mixture is smooth. Stir in eggs, one at a time. Stir in the dry ingredients. Mix in the chocolate chips. (It's OK if the chips start to melt slightly.)

Bake 30 minutes or until a tester inserted in the center comes out clean. Check after about 20 minutes. Remove and cool to room temperature. Cut into 16 large squares or 32 small ones. Store the bars in an airtight container at room temperature up to 3 days.

Note from Rob Wall: Ghiradelli's Double Dark Chocolate Chips, available at many supermarkets, are good in these bars. They are intensely chocolate in flavor and slightly larger than regular chips.

Submitted by Rob Wall – Chef for Team Rahal, Michigan International Speedway – Used with permission of MIS

Pancake Mix Cookie Bars

It's amazing what you can do with a box of pancake mix.

2 cups pancake or bisquick mix
1 1/4 cups brown sugar
3 eggs, beaten
1/4 cup flaked coconut
1 cup chopped walnuts or pecans
Powdered sugar

Combine all ingredients except powdered sugar in a bowl. Mix well, and pour into a greased and floured 9x11-inch cake pan. Smooth out to make even bars. Bake in a 325° oven about 30 minutes. Remove and top with powdered sugar. Allow to cool before slicing with a pizza cutter.

Submitted by Danny C. (and his mom) – Jimmy Spencer fan

Deck Chef Tip!

Batter up!

You could make pancake mix ahead and store it in an empty milk jug or other closed container. That way you can save leftover mix for the next day. Just be sure to keep the mix cold. Leave some extra space in each container, so if you get to the track and find your batter to be too thick, you could add water or milk, then seal and shake.

Caramel Brownies

1 (18¼-ounce) box chocolate cake mix
¾ cup butter, melted
⅓ cup evaporated milk
1½ cups butterscotch chips
1 cup chopped nuts
½ container caramel ice cream topping

Combine everything except the topping. Cook in a greased cake pan at 350° until center is firm. Remove from oven, poke a few holes in the brownie and cover with caramel topping. Cut and serve.

Peanut Butter Brownie Sandwiches

We like this because it is so easy and we can make it without a stove or oven.

2 boxes individually wrapped brownies
Peanut butter
1 can pre-made vanilla cake icing

Open all of the brownies, and place half of them along the bottom of a large cake pan. Top with a layer of peanut butter and then a layer of icing. Top with remaining brownies, then more peanut butter and icing. Cut and serve.

Submitted by Kellie and James – Lexington, Kentucky

Pumpkin Spice Cake with Cinnamon Cream Cheese Frosting

CAKE:

1 (15-ounce) can pumpkin purée
1 teaspoon ground cinnamon
1 teaspoon ground cloves
1 teaspoon ground nutmeg
1 (18.25-ounce) package yellow cake mix with pudding
¼ cup vegetable oil
2 eggs
1 teaspoon vanilla extract

Preheat oven to 350°. Grease and flour a 9x13-inch baking pan. Whisk together pumpkin, cinnamon, cloves and nutmeg. Set aside. In large bowl, mix together cake mix and oil. Beat in eggs, then fold in pumpkin mixture. Stir in vanilla. Pour batter into prepared pan. Bake 40 minutes, or until a toothpick inserted into center of cake comes out clean. Allow to cool.

FROSTING:

½ cup butter, softened
4 (3-ounce) packages cream cheese, softened
2 cups powdered sugar
1 teaspoon ground cinnamon
1 teaspoon vanilla extract

Cream together butter and cream cheese until light and fluffy. Beat in powdered sugar, mixing until smooth. Stir in cinnamon and vanilla. Spread Frosting over cooled cake.

Submitted by Megan L. Gill – Dover International Speedway

Piña Colada Cake

1 (18¼-ounce) package yellow cake mix
1 (15-ounce) can crushed pineapple, drained
1 (14-ounce) can cream of coconut
1 (14-ounce) can sweetened condensed milk
1 (12-ounce) container Cool Whip
1 (7-ounce) bag flaked coconut

Bake cake in a 9x13-inch pan according to the directions on box, except add pineapple to the mix. While cake is cooling, punch holes all over the cake with a drinking straw. Pour cream of coconut and sweetened condensed milk over top. Refrigerate cake overnight.

Spread Cool Whip on top of cake, and sprinkle with coconut.

Submitted by Tony Taffar – Gasman/Cook
#16 Naturally Fresh USAR Hooters Pro Cup Series

Michael Ritch checks things out under the hood before a race.

Mike Chambers

Driver – Stock, Late Model, Weekly
www.techracing.com

Mike Chambers' career in racing began at the youthful age of four. When most young boys dream of being firefighters and policemen, Mike was dreaming of being a NASCAR champion. When only eight years old, he was in the shop learning everything he could about a race car.

At the age of 15, Mike started racing go-karts, then medium stocks. In 1995, Mike attended the Richard Petty Driving Experience at the Lowe's Motor Speedway in Charlotte, North Carolina, to prepare him for his jump to stock cars. After reaching speeds of over 142 mph, he was placed in the top five of the speed charts.

Mike continued racing in the Pure Stock Division at Orange County in 1996, securing six front-row starts, two poles, two runner-up finishes, and nine top-fives, while finishing third in the points battle.

Mike felt the need for a greater challenge, so he made the move to the Limited Sportsman Division in 1998. He posted three front-row starts, one win, three top-threes, and seven top-five finishes earning him the third position in the points standings his rookie season. Even more impressive was the fact that Mike only missed winning the championship by a mere two points after leading them for over half of the season.

Not only does Mike drive the racecar, he is very knowledgeable about the setup and fabrication. In the future, Mike has his sights set on wins, while pursuing his dream of racing in the NASCAR NEXTEL Cup Series by advancing up the racing ladder.

Banana Cake

During any given race weekend, many rescue workers and police show up to make sure nobody gets hurt, and if they do, there is proper medical care available. This recipe comes from Steve, who has worked rescue at races from drag strips to dirt tracks and superspeedways.

3 bananas, thinly sliced
1 (18¼-ounce) box yellow cake mix
1 (3-ounce) box vanilla pudding
4 eggs, beaten
1 cup water
½ cup oil
½ cup chopped walnuts
½ cup brown sugar

In a large bowl, combine all ingredients. Cook in a greased and coated Bundt pan about 45–50 minutes at 350°.

Submitted by Steve L. – Volunteer rescue worker and race fan

Wacky Cake

This is a simple recipe that you can mix and bake in the same pan.

3 cups flour
2 cups sugar
6 tablespoons cocoa powder
2 teaspoons baking soda
½ teaspoon salt
½ cup oil
2 tablespoons vinegar
2 teaspoons vanilla
2 cups cold water

In an ungreased 9x13-inch nonstick cake pan, sift all dry ingredients together. Make 3 holes of graduated sizes in pile of dry ingredients. In the largest hole, put the oil; in the medium hole, put the vinegar; in the smallest hole, put the vanilla. Cover all with the 2 cups cold water. Using a fork, stir well, making sure all dry ingredients are mixed well. Bake at 350° for 25 minutes.

Submitted by Linda Renninger – Dover International Speedway

Moist Chocolate Cake

Made with hot coffee.

2 cups sugar
2 cups flour
1 teaspoon baking powder
2 teaspoons baking soda
½ teaspoon salt
⅔ cup cocoa powder
1 cup milk
½ cup salad oil (applesauce can be substituted)
1 teaspoon vanilla
2 eggs
1 cup hot coffee

Beat all ingredients except hot coffee together till mixed well. Add hot coffee and mix. Batter will be very runny. Bake at 350° for 35 minutes.

Submitted by Linda Renninger – Dover International Speedway

Jake Says—

Any slice of cake can be made better with a scoop of ice cream or topped with some fruit slices.

Molten Chocolate Cakes

Much thanks to Michelle and Jamie Melvin at Dover International Speedway for this wonderful recipe. Take a look at the directions for some of their notes on egg substitutes and semisweet chocolate, then enjoy some fantastic cake!

2 tablespoons butter, melted
2 tablespoons unsweetened cocoa
¾ cup butter, cut into pieces
3 (4-ounce) premium semisweet chocolate baking bars, broken into chunks (see note)
½ cup whipping cream
1¼ cups egg substitute (see note)
¾ cup sugar
⅔ cup all-purpose flour
Powdered sugar

Brush 16 muffin cups with 2 tablespoons melted butter. Sprinkle evenly with cocoa, shaking out excess. Place in refrigerator to firm butter. Place ¾ cup butter and chocolate in a large heavy saucepan. Cook over low heat, stirring often, until butter and chocolate melt. Slowly whisk in cream; set aside.

Combine egg substitute and sugar in a large mixing bowl. Beat at medium speed with an electric mixer 5–7 minutes or until slightly thickened. Add chocolate cream and flour; beat until blended. Pour batter into muffin cups, filling to about ¼ inch from tops. Cover and chill at least 1 hour or up to 24 hours.

Bake, uncovered, at 450° for 10–11 minutes or just until edges of cakes spring back when lightly touched, but centers are still soft. Let stand 3 minutes before loosening edges with a knife. Quickly invert cakes onto a baking sheet. Transfer to dessert plates using a spatula. Sprinkle with powdered sugar. Serve immediately. Yields 16 servings.

Note: Do not substitute semisweet chocolate morsels for the baking bars. You can usually find the baking bars in most stores alongside other baking chocolate. If not, look on the candy aisle. The recipe calls for egg substitute (instead of real eggs) because the cakes aren't in the oven long enough for eggs to cook thoroughly.

Submitted by Michelle and Jamie Melvin
Dover International Speedway

Cup of Strawberry Angel Food Cake

1 store-bought angel food cake
Large plastic cups
1 package strawberries, thawed
1 container sherbet
Whipped cream

Cut the cake into small pieces, and stuff the bottom of the cups with some cake. Top that with strawberries, sherbet and whipped cream. Serve with a plastic spoon.

Submitted by David and Lisa – Rusty Wallace / Michael Waltrip fans

Honey Pound Cake with Fruit

1 store-bought pound cake, sliced
2 tablespoons honey
1 container whipped cream
1 bag frozen fruit, thawed

Place a slice of pound cake on a plate. Combine honey and whipped cream. Spoon onto pound cake. Top with fruit and serve.

Submitted by Elliot – Virginia – Tailgate chef

HEY RACE FANS, did you know that stock car racing began in the southern United States in the 1920s during the age of Prohibition (that's the time when selling or drinking alcohol was illegal in the United States)? Bootleggers would deliver illegally made booze from hidden stills to hundreds of markets across the southeastern United States. To avoid police, bootleggers would need to have fast cars and be great drivers. Eventually these bootleggers began to race against each other to see who was the best driver and who had the fastest car. The sport of stock car racing was born!

Easy Chocolate Chip Pie

A great pie recipe that can be made beforehand and brought to the tailgate. Use a large pie shell or individual smaller pie shells.

1 cup sugar
½ cup flour
2 eggs, beaten
1¼ sticks butter, melted
1 cup chocolate chips
½ cup butterscotch chips
¾ cup pecans
½ cup coconut
1 teaspoon vanilla
1 unbaked pie crust or individual pie crusts
Ice cream or whipped topping

Blend all of the ingredients together and spoon into the pie crust. Cook at 350° about 30 minutes (about 20 minutes if you use smaller pie shells) or until pie filling gets firm. Top with ice cream or whipped topping.

Deck Chef Tip!

Easy as pie

Frozen pies are a snap at the track. To grill a frozen apple pie, just cover the pie lightly with foil and follow the directions on the box. Treat your covered grill as you would an oven (if you don't have an RV with an oven). Frozen pies that do not have to be cooked can be kept cold on ice until needed.

Holly's Easy Key Lime Pie

An easy way to do Key lime at the track.

1 (12-ounce) container Cool Whip
1 (14-ounce) can condensed milk
⅓ cup lime juice
Green food coloring
1 (9-inch) pie crust

Mix all ingredients and pour into pie crust. Chill and allow to thicken before serving.

Submitted by Holly J. – Concord, NC – Race fan

Frozen Chocolate Key Lime Pie

1 frozen Key lime pie
8 popsicle sticks
1 bottle chocolate hard shell topping

If your pie has a whipped cream coating, you may want to neatly scrape it off. Slice the frozen pie into 8 equal pieces. As quickly as possible, coat each slice with the hard shell chocolate topping. Place on wax paper and freeze. If you desire, after the coating has hardened, add a layer of chocolate to the bottom of each piece. Put a popsicle stick in center of each piece. Serve frozen like a popsicle.

HEY RACE FANS, did you know NASCAR mandates the use of a head and neck restraint system commonly called the Hans Device? It is mandated for use in the NASCAR NEXTEL Cup Series, the NASCAR BUSCH series, the NASCAR Craftsman Truck Series as well as the Touring Series.

Terry Bradshaw

www.fitzbradshawracing.com

The NASCAR BUSCH garage area would not be complete without the booming voice and laugh of NFL hall-of-famer and FOX Broadcaster Terry Bradshaw. But on race weekends Bradshaw is more than a fan, he is part owner of three BUSCH Series teams under the heading of FitzBradshaw Racing.

Stock car racing is not just about cars going around in circles on race day. During this race weekend Terry and the FitzBradshaw Racing family were joined by their friends from St. Jude Children's Research Hospital to announce the new paint schemes for select BUSCH races.

"We hope that all of the people who enjoy this sport will help support St. Jude by going online and getting a Racing To Save Lives bracelet," Armando Fitz and Bradshaw said. According to NASCAR there are over 75 million fans. "The children of St. Jude need our help."

Terry is always happy to talk racing or sports with just about any fan. "We stop for nobody and we stop for everybody for a picture!" Terry bellows with a large smile while hugging two ladies for a quick photo on the way back to the garage.

OTHER DESSERTS

David and Lisa's RV Cherry Cobbler

2 (21-ounce) cans cherry pie filling
1 (18¼-ounce) package white cake mix
⅓ cup brown sugar
⅔ cup butter, melted
½ cup chopped pecans

Grease a 9x13-inch cake pan. Pour the cherry pie filling into the pan and spread evenly. Gently spread the cake mix over the top of the filling. Cover with the brown sugar and butter. Sprinkle with the pecans, and cook until cake mix turns golden brown.

Submitted by David and Lisa – Rusty Wallace / Michael Waltrip fans

Kat and MeMaw's Cobbler

¼ cup butter, melted
1 cup self-rising flour
¾ cup sugar
¾ cup milk
1 (21-ounce) can your favorite fruit pie filling

Grease a glass baking dish with melted butter. Combine the flour, sugar and milk and beat gently to mix. Pour in baking dish, holding some to the side. Top with fruit filling and remaining batter. Cook in a 375° oven until the crust turns golden brown.

Submitted by Katherine Spencer – East Ridge, TN

Real Vanilla Wafer Banana Pudding

¾ cup sugar, divided
⅓ cup flour
Dash of salt
3 eggs, separated
2 cups milk
½ teaspoon vanilla flavoring
1 box vanilla wafers
4–5 ripe bananas, sliced

Mix half of the sugar, flour and salt in top of double boiler. Blend in 3 egg yolks and milk. Cook uncovered over boiling water, stirring constantly for 10–12 minutes or until thickened. Remove from heat; stir in vanilla. Spread small amount of pudding on bottom of 1½-quart casserole; cover with layer of wafers and layer of sliced bananas. Pour about ⅓ of pudding over bananas. Continue to layer wafers, bananas and pudding to make a total of 3 layers each, ending with pudding. Beat egg whites until soft peaks form. Gradually add remaining ¼ cup sugar, beating until stiff but not dry. Spoon on top of pudding, spreading to cover entire surface and sealing well to edges. Bake at 350° for 15–20 minutes or until browned. You may enjoy warm, or refrigerate several hours. Makes 8 servings.

Submitted by Tim and Tammy Chambers – Tech Racing team owners

---

HEY RACE FANS, did you know that Dale Earnhardt, Dale Earnhardt, Jr. and Kerry Earnhardt only raced together on the same track once in NASCAR competition? This happened on August 20, 2000, at Michigan International Speedway during the Pepsi 400.

Instant Strawberry Pudding

This recipe was presented to me at about 2 o'clock in the morning on a road trip to and from a race. You can meet some really nice people late at night in a Waffle House outside of racetracks. The couple next to me were also weary race fans and they offered up three really easy dessert recipes and a few great stories best suited for a different book!

2 (3-ounce) boxes vanilla instant pudding
Milk as needed for pudding
1 cup diced strawberries
Whipped cream topping

Make the pudding as directed on the box. Stir in strawberries. Serve chilled, topped with whipped cream.

Submitted by David and Lisa – Rusty Wallace / Michael Waltrip fans

Strawberry Chocolate Pudding

This is a great way to make any flavor pudding a treat.

2 (3-ounce) boxes instant chocolate pudding
Milk
1 box frozen strawberries

Make the pudding as per the directions, less about 1/4 of the milk, because the strawberries add some liquids to it and you don't want it to be runny! In a blender, mash the strawberries, then add to the pudding and stir. Serve chilled, topped with fresh fruit or whipped cream.

Note: Barbara says you can also use vanilla pudding with pineapple or bananas and coconut. "It's easy and you can make all kinds of neat flavors."

Submitted by Kev and Barbara – NASCAR fans

KC Racing Graphics

Chattanooga, Tennessee
423-698-7234

Kathie Coulter was born into the sport of racing. "It's something my whole family has been involved in since before I was born." So it just stands to reason that somehow Kathie would find her niche in the sport. "Have you ever wondered where all of those cool designs come from on the cars you see heading around the track every weekend? That's what I do. I make designs for everything from small team race cars, to haulers and more." According to Kathie, her skill at designing racing graphics has not gone unnoticed by other customers. "It has grown a bit, and is still growing."

Kathie says her customers are now coming from not only the racing industry, but other areas as well. "I have designed schemes for everything from team uniforms, team shirts and hats, race cars and haulers to fire trucks!"

Of course, Kathie follows her dad's team around the asphalt racing series and when she is not with them, she heads to other races. "We race asphalt, my cousin races dirt tracks, and of course, we go to tracks like Bristol and such for Cup races."

So the next time you see a hauler drive by with a cool logo, a shirt with a neat design, or a car with some fantastic graphics, you may be looking at one of Kathie's designs. "I hope people like them. I always try to do something cool looking and eye-catching."

Maggie's Cherry Dessert

1 cup ricotta cheese
1 cup powdered sugar
¼ cup sour cream
¼ cup coffee liqueur
1 tablespoon cinnamon
1½ cups shortbread cookie crumbs (about 30 cookies)
1 (21-ounce) can cherry filling and topping
Grated chocolate

In a large mixing bowl, combine ricotta cheese, powdered sugar, sour cream, coffee liqueur and cinnamon, and mix well. Crush the cookies until almost a powder. Spoon equal amounts of ricotta mixture, cookies and pie filling into a glass and repeat. Top with grated chocolate, and chill for several hours before serving. This makes about 7–8 servings.

Submitted by Elliot – Virginia – Tailgate Chef

Deck Chef Tip!

Super bowl

If you are looking for a good dessert but lack a good fridge to chill items, then don't overlook packages of premade Jell-O and puddings. Just add fruit, whipped cream and other items for a perfect dessert with a bowl you can throw away!

Dump Salad

1 (21-ounce) can cherry pie filling
1 (14-ounce) can condensed milk
1 cup chopped pecans
1 cup mini marshmallows
1 (8-ounce) can crushed pineapple, drained
1 (12-ounce) container Cool Whip

Mix the pie filling and condensed milk together. Add pecans, marshmallows and pineapple. Mix well. Fold in the Cool Whip.

Submitted by Tony Taffar – Gasman/Cook
#16 Naturally Fresh USAR Hooters Pro Cup Series

Grilled Apples

An easy recipe for a great snack.

4 apples
Peanut butter
Brown sugar
Honey

Slice apples and place on the grill for a few minutes. Combine some peanut butter with brown sugar and honey. Mix well. Spread over apple slices, and serve warm.

Submitted by Lori F. – SAS / NASCAR race fan

Speedway Coffee Cake and Ice Cream

1 box Little Debbie Coffee Cakes
½ gallon French vanilla ice cream
1 bottle chocolate hard shell topping

Open coffee cakes and top with ice cream. Cover with hard shell topping. Allow topping to get hard, then serve.

Submitted by David and Lisa – Rusty Wallace / Michael Waltrip fans

Kent's Stuffed Muffin Sundays

I suggest making the muffins in your kitchen before the tailgate and just warming them up on-site. But if you can't warm them up, don't worry about it . . . they still taste great!

1 box blueberry muffin mix
Water or milk as needed for mix
Your favorite ice cream
Sliced fruit of choice (optional)

Make muffins as per directions on box. While still hot, remove top and scoop out a bit of the center. Fill the hole with a scoop of your favorite ice cream; lay top of muffin back on top. Don't worry, it will fall over a bit. Garnish with some sliced fruit, if desired.

Hot Fudge Ice Cream Bar Dessert

This recipe was given to me by Debbie Stewart, whose husband Greg is a crew member for Andy Belmont Racing. Thanks to Sandra Shipley of Hixson Motorsports for hooking me up with a great dessert from the garage area!

1 (16-ounce) can chocolate syrup
¾ cup peanut butter
19 ice cream sandwiches (or enough to make 2 layers)
1 (12-ounce) container frozen whipped topping
1 cup salted peanuts

Pour the chocolate syrup into a medium microwave-safe bowl, microwave 2 minutes on HIGH. Do not allow to boil. Stir peanut butter into hot chocolate with whisk until smooth. Allow to cool to room temperature.

Line the bottom of a 9x13-inch dish with ice cream sandwiches; spread half the whipped topping over the sandwiches. Spoon half the chocolate mixture over that. Top with half the peanuts. Repeat layers. Freeze until firm, about 1 hour. Cut in squares and serve.

Submitted by Debbie Stewart and Greg Stewart
South Bend, IN – Andy Belmont Racing

Deep-Fried Twinkies

I know, this sounds like a way to knock a few years off your life. But it's GOOD!

1 box Twinkies
Wooden skewers
2 cups store-bought pancake mix
⅓ cup brown sugar
Oil for frying
Powdered sugar

Remove Twinkies from the package. Skewer with wooden skewers. Prepare pancake batter per box, but add brown sugar. Coat Twinkies with a thin layer of batter, then deep-fry. Just do a few at a time. Cover with powdered sugar, or try topping with chocolate syrup, maple syrup, whipped cream and nuts (served like a banana split). A real diet killer, but fun!

Talk about a quick checkup! Just goes to show you that a dedicated team member can work on a car just about anywhere, any time and any place!

Honey Bars with Ice Cream

¼ cup honey
¼ cup butter
1 tablespoon cinnamon
Dash of ginger
4 cups mini-marshmallows
6 cups favorite bran cereal
1 cup peanuts
Your favorite ice cream

Mix honey, butter, cinnamon and ginger in a large saucepan, and melt over low heat. Add marshmallows, then stir in cereal and peanuts until everything is well coated. Grease a 9x13-inch pan, and spoon the mixture into it. Allow to cool, then cut into squares. Serve with a scoop of your favorite ice cream.

Submitted by Elliot – Virginia – Tailgate chef

Bourbon Chocolate Dessert Sauce

This is a great sauce for all kinds of desserts.

2 tablespoons bourbon
½ cup sugar
¼ cup cocoa
1½ tablespoons cornstarch
½ cup evaporated skim milk
2 teaspoons vanilla flavoring

In a small pan, combine bourbon, sugar, cocoa and cornstarch; stir in evaporated milk. Cook over low heat and stir constantly until it thickens a bit. Remove from heat, and add vanilla. Add more cocoa and sugar, if desired.

Submitted by Belinda W. – Professional caterer and race fan

HEY RACE FANS, did you know that Talladega Superspeedway was molded out of a soybean field located next to a couple of abandoned World War II airport runways, and was opened in September of 1969?

RACING 101

When my son Macee started going to races with me, I realized that even though he knew who drove which cars, he was blissfully unaware of some basic racing info. Then when Ally joined us for a few laps around the track, she asked some of the same questions about common terms, flags and such. So I decided this chapter of racing definitions, a guide to racing flags, and info about some great racetracks was in order. Now keep in mind that things change. The sport of stock car racing is known for changing things mid-season. The info in this chapter is as up to date as possible and comes from official media quides from different series, tracks and organizations. I suggest before going to any track, check for changes in parking, tailgating and camping regulations.

RACING DICTIONARY

[Words Ya Gotta Know]

Many of these terms apply to all forms of racing, but you may hear the majority of them during a stock car race. Like any other sport or job, motorsports has a language all to itself. Here is a short list of terms you may or may not hear around the track.

AIR DAM: Not like a dam that holds water. An air dam helps keep stock cars on the track. It's that thing on the front of the car below the bumper. A downforce is created when air is forced over the top of the car.

AERO PUSH: Aero push is most often heard around the NASCAR circuit because of the design of the cars. When one car gets behind another car in corners, the airflow is disrupted causing the car to get loose. This most often happens around turns.

APRON: I know, in cooking an apron is that funny thing we wear with catch phrases such as "Kiss the Chef" printed on the front. In racing, an apron is the bottom area of the racetrack. In many racing series, thanks to NASCAR, you can't advance your position by going below the yellow line onto the apron.

BALANCE: To a stock car, dirt track or any race fan, balance is a critical thing. In fact many great race-day stories involve balance. "Ya shud-da seen Billy when he lost his balance . . . " On the track balance is simple, everything is working and the car seems to drive itself around the track. It's balanced.

BANKING: Often seen around the ATM's during a race weekend. "Gotta do a bit of bankin' before the flag drops!" Banking is also the slope of a racetrack found most often in the turns. The banking helps keep the cars from sliding up and off the track. The banking of a track is measured from the edge of the apron to the edge of the out-side wall.

DIRTY AIR: Again, several terms apply: the scent of the air too near the restrooms or concession stand garbage; the air coming from your neighbors campsite. But in racing, it means the turbulent air used and discarded by the lead car.

DRAFT: This one is simple—cold beer. Or the aerodynamic effect that happens when two or more cars are traveling nose-to-tail. This allows the cars "in the draft" to run faster than a single car. Plain and simple, the lead car or cars in the draft burn all of their fuel pushing the air away. Cars behind this car can follow in its wake of clean air.

DOWNFORCE: Downforce is very important. It is the pressure, like a weight, on top of the race car. A car with good downforce has a better grip on the racetrack going into, through and out of the turns.

DOUGHNUT: You might eat a couple of the sugar or powdered kind for breakfast before the race, but during a race, a doughnut is different. A doughnut is the round mark a tire from one car leaves on the paint job of another car when they rub. Doughnuts can be by accident or given on purpose.

FUEL CELL: A holding tank for a race car's gas. Fuel cells are different from a gas tank. A fuel cell is a high tech spin-off from the aerospace industry. A fuel cell consists of a metal box around a flexible bladder and foam baffling, designed to be as damage proof as possible.

GROOVE: In the infield, a groove is often the result of some pre-race concerts. On the track, a groove is the fastest line a car can take around the track. You can see the groove because it is covered with tread way and skid marks. If you see an aerial shot of the track on TV, look for the dark line around the track. That's the groove.

HAPPY HOUR: Again, in the infield parking areas and the campgrounds, happy hour starts at about beer thirty or a quarter past whiskey. On the track, happy hour is the last practice session held before a race.

HANDLING: You may end up saying something like, "How's he handling the wreck?" to a friend when a another buddy's driver smacks the wall during the race. But handling is the term used to describe how a car is driving during practice, qualifying and the race.

INTERVAL: The time it takes you to get to the concession stand or to the restroom and back to your seat during a race. Also, the timed-distance between two cars.

LAP TRAFFIC: Lap traffic means faster cars in front have caught up with slower cars in the back and have to start weaving in and out to pass them and keep up the pace to stay ahead.

LOOSE: Do not use this term to describe any of your neighbors in a race camper city. In a quick sense, loose is opposite of tight. Being loose happens when a car's rear tires lose grip with the racetrack. Loose is when a driver comes off the gas a bit in a turn and the car starts to slide sideways back end first.

MARBLES: Your friend may have lost his marbles for liking the driver he does, but here is what marbles are in racing. Marbles are bits of rubber that wear off tires and collect high on the racetrack above the groove. When heated tires run over this loose stuff, it can cause cars to slide just like stepping on kids' marbles and busting your rear! Drivers wiggle their cars back and forth during caution laps to knock off marbles they may have collected.

POLE POSITION: The car that starts at the very front of the starting grid. Pole position is awarded to the fastest car during qualifying.

PIT ROAD (a.k.a. Pit Row): The area where pit crews service the cars. At most tracks, access to pit road is limited. Pits are generally located along the inside of the front straight-a-way on larger tracks. On many short tracks, because of space limitations, pit roads may be located on the front and back straightaways.

PIT STALL: The designated area along pit road which a team can use during pit stops. Each car stops in the team's stall before being serviced.

RESTRICTOR PLATE: A restrictor plate is a metal plate that is placed between the carburetor and the engine's intake manifold. It has four holes drilled in it. The plate is designed to reduce the flow of air and fuel which decreases horsepower which slows the car down a bit. Some racetracks require this for safety purposes. Restrictor plates were implemented in 1988 following Bobby Allison's crash into a retaining fence at 210 mph, which endangered hundreds of fans.

SCUFFS: Tires used at least once to take the factory glaze off them, but still saved for more racing. Scuffing tires for a lap gets them heated and hardens the compound, keeping them consistent when they're put back on for the race. It can also mean the marks on your knees if you trip over something in the campground area.

SETUP: Yes, it does apply to how you have your spot "set up" for the big day—flags, coolers, lawn chairs, stereos and such. It's also how a car's engine, suspension, aerodynamics and tires are adjusted to handle on a particular racetrack.

SHORT TRACK: Short tracks are considered to be racetracks that are shorter than one mile in length.

SPOILER: No, it's not your ex-spouse calling about five minutes before the green flag. The spoiler is a strip of aluminum that stretches across the width of a race vehicle's rear deck. It is designed to create downforce on the rear of the car.

SPOTTER: A spotter can be your buddy keeping an eye out for good-looking people of the opposite sex, or a spotter can be a race-team member stationed above the grandstand who is a driver's second pair of eyes. Spotters use radios to speak with a driver during a race and help direct the driver around wrecks, or lap traffic coming up.

SUPERSPEEDWAY: Superspeedways are often called this if the track is two miles or longer.

STICKERS: Stickers are brand new tires with stickers often still on them from the factory.

TEMPLATE: A measuring device used to check the body shape and size to ensure the car complies to body shape rules.

TIGHT: When a car is too tight, it is hard to drive, because the front tires don't grip the track surface and start sliding up out of the groove. Getting "tight" or having the car push often happens when going into or out of a turn.

TRI-OVAL: A racetrack that has a fifth turn.

VICTORY LANE: Where we all want to end up in our racing fantasies. Victory lane is the same as the winner's circle.

HEY RACE FANS, did you know that corporate branding of the NASCAR Series on a large scale began in 1971 when the R. J. Reynolds Tobacco Company became the sponsor? The series was then called NASCAR Winston Cup. Then there was the NASCAR Winston West Series and the NASCAR Winston Racing Series, which is now the NASCAR Dodge Weekly Series.

DECK CHEF GUIDE TO RACING FLAGS

Racing flags are a traditional way to communicate information about the track, track conditions, race conditions and wrecks to drivers and crews. Today flags are still used by every racing series in addition to onboard warning systems, radio communication and lights along the track to signal green flag, yellow flag and red flag conditions. Here is a basic breakdown of what these flags and their colors and patterns mean.

GREEN: The green flag is a simple one. It means the track is clear and all race cars can put the pedal to the metal. This flag is used to signal the beginning of the race and any restarts.

YELLOW (CAUTION): The yellow flag is also one almost every race fan knows. It means that the track is not clear and you should slow down. The drivers should also hold their position behind the pace car. Most often the yellow flag is shown after an accident or if there are other problems such as wrecked car parts on the track.

RED: The red flag means STOP. This flag is waved when something has happened to make conditions not only unsafe to race at normal racing speeds, but also unsafe to even continue around the track. Cars follow the lead of the pace car and come to a complete stop.

WHITE: The white flag means there is only one more lap to go!

BLUE WITH YELLOW STRIPE: This means several things, but most often it means take a look in your mirrors because there are faster cars coming up behind you.

BLACK: The black flag is often waved at specific cars. Most commonly the cars are instructed to head to the pits for consultation, either to take a penalty stop-and-go or because the car has become unsafe and can't maintain an appropriate speed.

RED AND BLACK COMBO: Waving the red flag and the black flag together means a practice session has ended. All cars must come to a stop and return to their pits or to the garage area.

BLACK WITH WHITE CROSS: If a car is shown a black flag and the driver or team does not respond, they are then shown a black and white cross flag, which means they are no longer being scored until they acknowledge the black flag.

CHECKERED: Most of us know this one, but just in case you don't, the checkered flag signals that the race has reached its scheduled distance and the first car there wins the race! ". . . and there goes the checkered flag!"

Even after a wreck and some heavy damage, the Coulter team was able to hold off other cars to take the checkered flag.

Rick Coulter

Race Car Builder
Chattanooga, Tennessee
423-698-7234

"When I was about ten years old, I was in my front yard riding my bike. A truck pulled by the house pulling a race car. It was so nice looking. Ever since then I knew what I wanted to do." That's how Rick Coulter of Coulter Racing describes his intro into the racing industry. He describes it with passion.

That passion has led to a lifetime of learning how to build race cars. "Every year, the cars get better and faster. We keep building them."

Rick builds cars for his own team, other teams, for sale and for rent. "I really never wanted to be a driver. I always wanted to build the car. I always wanted to make the fastest car."

According to Rick, the cars have a special place with him. "I can remember the first one I ever built. It was really stock then. I cut some stuff, added some things, did the springs . . . that was a car." Today the cars are intricate combinations of tubing, metals, panels and motors all formed to fit the series the car will be running in.

"Things are different today. But I have made a job out of a hobby. That's fun," Rick says with a smile as he looks at a car suspended above our heads in his shop.

RACETRACK QUICK FACTS

NASCAR, BUSCH, CRAFTSMAN TRUCK, ARCA, ASA

This is a quick list of tracks that host most NASCAR, BUSCH, CRAFTSMAN TRUCK, ARCA and ASA races. Many drivers compete in several of the different series. ALWAYS check with the individual track to determine rules on exposed cooking flames, camping and other tailgating restrictions. Almost every track allows some sort of outdoor cooking. But due to ever changing local fire regulations and the liability issue, tracks are often forced to rewrite camping rules. Also, private campsites near the track will often have completely different rules. Just check the regulations before you head to the track. Due to the explosion of interest in motorsports, track owners and campground owners usually now list all regulations and restrictions on their websites. A great idea is to subscribe to your favorite track's email newsletter if they offer one. And remember, there are MANY more fantastic and fun racetracks across the country that offer competitive racing. Stop by your local facility to experience the excitement of motorsports firsthand!

Note: *Track information is as up to date as possible. Due to series date and track changes, always check with the track you plan to visit for a complete listing of events. All information is taken from official press kits, media guides, publications from different series, and the National Speedway Directory. The National Speedway Directory lists over 1700 tracks, racing museums, sanctioning bodies, racing publications and more.*

Atlanta Motor Speedway

Many fans in racing consider Atlanta to be one of the best facilities to see a race.

Series: NASCAR, BUSCH, ARCA, ASA

www.atlantamotorspeedway.com

1500 Highway 19-41 South

Hampton, GA 30228

Tickets & Info: 770-946-4211

TRACK FACTS

Distance: 1.54 miles

Degree of Banking in Turns: 24 degrees

Degree of Banking in Straights: 5 degrees

Shape: D-shape oval

Camping and Tailgating: Atlanta Motor Speedway offers several on-site campgrounds for reserved and unreserved camping. Each has easy access to the track. They also allow open flame grills and barrel cooking. All grills and barrels must be removed after each event. No golf carts allowed. Call for more information.

PHOTO BY JOE NORMAN

Campers and RVs fill the campgrounds outside of Atlanta Motor Speedway the night before a race.

Bristol Motor Speedway

Considered by many to be the hardest ticket in racing, Bristol is a track that many drivers, and their teams, say is designed to destroy cars.

Series: NASCAR, BUSCH, ASA, HOOTERS PRO CUP, Drag

www.bristolmotorspeedway.com

151 Speedway Boulevard

Bristol, TN 37620

Tickets & Info: 423-764-1161

TRACK FACTS

Distance: .533 miles

Degree of Banking in Turns: 36 degrees

Degree of Banking in Straights: 16 degrees

Shape: Oval short track

Camping & Tailgating: They call it the hardest ticket in NASCAR and it also applies to camping and tailgating. BMS owns a camping area but availability is VERY limited. Visit the Bristol Motor Speedway website for links and contact info for many fantastic camping areas just down the road from the speedway. Each campground has different rules for open flame and cooking. Many offer shuttle services.

California Speedway

This speedway offers race fans the superspeedway race with the feel of a short track. Plenty of great seats, food, and many fan-friendly extras.

Series: NASCAR, BUSCH, Grand Am, IRL, AMA

www.californiaspeedway.com

9300 Cherry Avenue

Fontana, CA 92335

Tickets & Info: 1-800-944-7223

TRACK FACTS

Distance: 2.0 miles

Degree of Banking in Turns: 14 degrees

Degree of Banking in Front Strech: 11 degrees

Degree of Banking in Back Stretch: 3 degrees

Shape: D-shaped oval with road course

Track Surface: Asphalt

Camping & Tailgating: California Speedway offers RV infield camping. You can call for information and space availability at 1-800-367-3687. The track offers ticketed fans several areas to take advantage of race-day fun, including their "Party Zone."

Chicagoland Speedway

Just outside of the Windy City in Joliet, Chicagoland Speedway offers race fans and teams a first-rate facility to drive, or just simply enjoy the race.

Series: NASCAR, BUSCH, ARCA, ASA

www.chicagolandspeedway.com

500 Speedway Boulevard

Joliet, IL 60433

Tickets & Info: 815-727-RACE

TRACK FACTS

Distance: 1.5 miles

Degree of Banking in Turns: 18 degrees

Degree of Banking in Tri Oval: 11 degrees

Degree of Banking in Back Stretch: 5 degrees

Shape: Tri-oval

Camping & Tailgating: RV camping both infield and outside track with several levels of availability and pricing. The Chicagoland website is full of information. Open fires are allowed in above ground grills. No golf carts allowed. Private camping also is available nearby.

HEY RACE FANS, did you know that the Chicagoland facility is so large, sitting on 930 acres of land, that it could hold 42 United Centers, which is home to the Chicago Bulls and Blackhawks?

Darlington Raceway

Just between a speedway and a short track. Lots of seating and good views throughout.

Series: NASCAR, BUSCH, ARCA, ASA, CRAFTSMAN

www.darlingtonraceway.com

1301 Harry Byrd Highway

Darlington, SC 29532

Tickets & Info: 843-395-8499

TRACK FACTS

Distance: 1.366 miles

Degree of Banking in Turns: 25 degrees turns 1 & 2

Degree of Banking in Turns: 23 degrees turns 3 & 4

Degree of Banking in Straights: 6 degrees

Shape: Oval (egg shape)

Camping & Tailgating: Darlington offers infield and outside RV reserved parking and camping areas. And as of 2004, tent camping has returned to the track in select areas. Call the ticket office for availability and prices.

HEY RACE FANS, did you know that Darlington was laid out with one set of turns more narrow than the other? The reason for the design was that when Harold Brasington started moving dirt around the old peanut farm, he wanted to protect a favorite pond named Ramsey's Pond. They track layout was changed in 1997, when the southern straightaway of the track became the front stretch.

Daytona International Speedway

They say this is where it all started! To many fans, Daytona is the place you have to visit at least once during the sports speed week. Tons of racing, tons of fan-friendly events and lots of great tailgating.

Series: NASCAR, BUSCH, CRAFTSMAN Truck, ARCA

www.daytonaintlspeedway.com

1801 West International Speedway Boulevard

Daytona Beach, FL 32114

Tickets & Info: 1-800-PIT-SHOP or 386-253-RACE

TRACK FACTS

Distance: 2.5 miles

Degree of Banking in Turns: 31 degrees

Degree of Banking in Tri-Oval: 18 degrees

Degree of Banking in Straight: 3 degrees

Shape: Tri-oval and road course

Camping & Tailgating: Daytona International offers several levels of specialty-vehicle parking all around the complex. Camping and tailgating options on-site and nearby are best found out by calling the ticket office. And check the Visitor Center for area camping and RV options. When inside the facility, fans can carry several items including a small under-seat cooler, etc. But these can change per event due to security measures.

Dover International Speedway

Race fans and drivers call it the Monster Mile. This one-mile oval is well known for its exciting races filled with lots of bumping and grinding. Great seats and fan friendly.

Series: NASCAR, BUSCH, BUSCH North, NASCAR Craftsman Truck

www.doverspeedway.com

1131 North DuPont Highway

Dover, DE 19901

Tickets & Info: 302-734-RACE or 1-800-441-RACE

TRACK FACTS

Distance: 1 mile

Degree of Banking in Turns: 24 degrees

Degree of Banking in Straights: 9 degrees

Shape: Oval

Camping & Tailgating: Dover offers many options for RV campers. Tent camping is not allowed and ground fires are not permitted. Propane grills are permitted. General safety rules apply. The fans are treated to a vast amount of fun while on the facility, including several restaurants and more! They do allow under-seat coolers and clear carry bags.

Will your favorite driver be the one to tame the Monster Mile? Dover International Speedway is a great place to see a NASCAR race; there isn't a bad seat in the house.

Gateway International Raceway

Gateway International, just outside of St. Louis, offers extremely long straights that head into complete half ovals. It is hard to say that there is a turn 1 & 2 or a turn 3 & 4 since they just blend into each other. Fancy footwork, brakes, gears and the gas make for some tight races.

Series: BUSCH, ARCA, NHRA, NASCAR Craftsman

www.gatewayraceway.com

700 Raceway Boulevard

Madison, IL 62060

Tickets & Info 618-875-7550 or 1-866-35-SPEED

TRACK FACTS

Distance: 1.25 miles

Degree of Banking in Turns 1 & 2: 11 degrees

Degree of Banking in Turns 3 & 4: 9 degrees

Degree of Banking in Straights: 2 degrees

Shape: Oval

Camping & Tailgating: RV and car race-weekend passes are sold through the ticket office. Call for availability.

Homestead - Miami Speedway

Located outside of Miami in Homestead, this track offers fans everything from sun to a tropical breeze. Oh yeah, the racing is pretty darned good as well. Homestead takes advantage of the superspeedway with great banking! Always an exciting race.

Series: NASCAR, BUSCH, IRL, INDY, Rolex

www.racemiami.com

One Speedway Boulevard

Homestead, FL 33035-1501

Tickets & Info: 305-230-7223

TRACK FACTS

Distance: 1.5 miles

Degree of Banking in Turns: 20 degrees

Degree of Banking in Straights: 4 degrees

Shape: Oval and road course

Camping & Tailgating: RV Camping is allowed for RV campers. Space is limited and reserved. Call the speedway for more information.

Indianapolis Motor Speedway

Home of the Brickyard 500 and of course the Indy 500. This track probably has more history than any other—more than can be written here. The website for the track is very informative. In 1909, over 3.2 million paving bricks were laid on the track to provide a better racing surface. That's where the nickname "The Brickyard" comes from.

www.brickyard.com

4790 W. 16th Street

Indianapolis, IN 46222

Tickets & Info: 1-800-822-4639

TRACK FACTS

Distance: 2.5 miles

Degree of Banking in Turns: 9 degrees

Shape: Squared oval

Camping & Tailgating: Seven camping and RV areas are available around the facility. State law does not permit open ground fires. Basic safety rules apply. The track offers camping for most events and race weekends including the Indy 500, the Brickyard 400, and the United States Grand Prix. Call the ticket office for complete information. A wide variety of services are available nearby from stores to restaurants and even auto repair—so you won't feel stuck.

Indianapolis Raceway Park

A very nice short track that offers drivers a different feel due to the low degree of banking in the turns. Located just outside of Indianapolis, this track offers many fan-friendly accommodations seen at larger facilities.

Series: BUSCH, NASCAR Craftsman Truck, NHRA, Mac Tools International

www.irponline.com

10267 East U.S. Highway 136

Indianapolis Raceway Park, IN 46234

Tickets & Info: 1-800-884-6472

TRACK FACTS

Distance: .686 miles

Degree of Banking in Turns: 12 degrees

Degree of Banking in Straights: 2 degrees

Shape: Oval, drag and road course

Camping & Tailgating: RV parking for select events is permitted. Contact the ticket office for a complete list of events and fees. There is no tent camping allowed on the facility grounds, but you can contact Raceview Campgrounds at 317-852-5737. (Raceview Campgrounds is not affiliated with IRP.)

Infineon Raceway

A beautiful place to see a race. This track offers race fans fantastic racing almost year round!

Series: NASCAR, BUSCH, NASCAR WEST, SCCA, NHRA, INDY and more

www.infineonraceway.com

Highways 37 and 121

Sonoma, CA 95476

Tickets & Info: 1-800-870-7223

TRACK FACTS

Distance: 1.99 miles

Degree of Banking in Turns: Varies

Shape: Road course

Camping: RV Camping with hookups. Wood or charcoal not allowed. Gas Grills and smokers allowed. Contact the ticket office for race weekend special events and availability.

HEY RACE FANS, did you know that Ricky Rudd won the inaugural NASCAR race at Infineon Raceway in 1989?

Kansas Speedway

Kansas Speedway is a wonderful track located just outside of Kansas City. Smell the barbecue! The facility has tons of room to expand seating and offers fans great views from the grandstands.

Series: NASCAR, BUSCH, CRAFTSMAN, NASCAR WEST, ARCA RE/MAX, INDY

www.kansasspeedway.com

701 Speedway Boulevard

Kansas City, KS 66111

Tickets & Info: 913-328-RACE

TRACK FACTS

Distance: 1.5 miles

Degree of Banking in Turns: 15 degrees

Degree of Banking in Front Stretch: 10.4 degrees

Degree of Banking in Back Stretch: 5 degrees

Shape: D-shaped tri-oval

Track Surface: Pavement

Camping & Tailgating: Kansas offers infield and outside-of-track RV camping with rates that vary per race weekend. There are three RV/camping areas. The official policy of Kansas Speedway is to encourage tailgates! This is from their media fan information. "Yes. We encourage our guests to get to the racetrack early. Parking lots open at 7 a.m., and grandstand gates open at 8 a.m. So tailgating is a good way to pass the time before the grandstand gates open. If you decide to tailgate, please leave all food and drink in your cars. Outside food or drink and bags larger than 6x6x12 inches are not allowed through the grandstand gates."

Kentucky Speedway

Kentucky Speedway is located about 45 minutes south of Cincinnati, Ohio, in Sparta, Kentucky. The track is very modern and is very fan friendly with tons of parking and RV parking.

Series: BUSCH, ARCA, ASA

www.kentuckyspeedway.com

4760 Sparta Pike

Sparta, KY 41086

Tickets & Info: 1-888-652-RACE

TRACK FACTS

Distance: 1.5 miles

Degree of Banking in Turns: 14 degrees

Degree of Banking in Straights: 8 degrees

Shape: D-shaped oval

Camping & Tailgating: Kentucky Speedway offers RV and event camping on a limited and reserved basis in the turns, about 200 spaces. A general RV camping area is also available on a first-come first-serve basis. It has over 1,000 spaces. Prices are very good and the general RV area is huge! There are also several private camping facilities just off the property. The Kentucky Speedway website has tones of area camping, dining info, etc. All track-owned camping areas offer free shuttles to the track. Due to local codes, restrictions may apply for open fires. Check with the ticket office for their latest guidelines. General tailgating and safety guidelines apply.

Las Vegas Motor Speedway

Fairly new, this track has quickly become a fan favorite. Located just outside of Las Vegas, the track is easy to get to, fan friendly and offers the obvious advantage of being near Vegas! The facility is huge with a paved oval, drag strip, dirt track and even facilities to host events such as rodeos.

Series: NASCAR, BUSCH, Craftsman, NHRA

www.lvms.com

7000 Las Vegas Boulevard

Las Vegas, Nevada 89115

Tickets & Info: 1-800-644-4444

TRACK FACTS

Distance: 1.5 miles

Degree of Banking in Turns: 12 degrees

Degree of Banking in front Stretch: 9 degrees

Degree of Banking in Back Stretch: 3 degrees

Shape: D-shaped oval paved, dirt, drag

Camping & Tailgating: Las Vegas Motor Speedway has RV spaces available in the infield and in a lot located behind the back-stretch and turn one of the speedway. Due to local fire codes, fires, fireworks and open fire-type grills are not allowed. Covered gas-style BBQ grills are allowed. The campgrounds do offer incredible ease to the speedway. They now enforce a quiet time from 11 p.m. to 7 a.m.

Lowe's Motor Speedway

Lowe's Motor Speedway is is often called stock car racing's "home track." Located just outside of Charlotte, North Carolina, in Concord, this facility caters to the fans, with races from many series. The facility now has a 15,000-seat dirt track and road course as well.

Series: NASCAR, BUSCH, ARCA, ASA, SAS, SCCA & more

www.lowesmotorspeedway.com

5555 Concord Parkway South

Concord, NC 28027

Tickets & Info: 704-455-3200 or 1-800-455-FANS

TRACK FACTS

Distance: 1.5 miles

Degree of Banking in Turns: 24 degrees

Degree of Banking in Straights: 5 degrees

Shape: Paved D-shaped oval

Camping & Tailgating: Lowe's Motor Speedway has RV spaces available in the infield and areas surrounding the speedway. Call the ticket office for information on purchasing camping space. The facilities are very impressive. Combined with local privately owned campgrounds, you could pretty much just tailgate, miss the race, and still have a great time. We are talking stocked ponds, picnic tables, grills, shuttles and more.

Martinsville Speedway

A granddaddy track on the stock car circuit. This facility opened its doors for racing two full years before NASCAR was founded.

Series: NASCAR, Craftsman

www.martinsvillespeedway.com

340 Speedway Road

Martinsville, VA 24112

Tickets & Info: 276-956-3151

TRACK FACTS

Distance: .526 miles

Degree of Banking in Turns: 12 degrees

Shape: Paved oval

Camping & Tailgating: Martinsville offers both RV and tent camping. The facilities are within easy access to the track. There are no hookups, but there is a dump station. For tent campers, shower and restroom facilities are on-site. Wood, charcoal and gas grills are permitted. Wood fires must be off ground. Same day general parking tailgating is permitted with picnic-style foods. No overnight parking is allowed in the general parking areas.

Rescue workers are always ready at the track.

Memphis Motorsports Park

A classic mid-length track with a short track feel. The Memphis Motorsports Park oval offers slight banking on the straights and a bit more in the turns. This forces teams to take a different approach to setting up their cars than if on a high-banked short track. Lots of seating, and near the casinos and attractions of Mississippi. Complete with Drag strip and dirt oval.

Series: BUSCH, Craftsman, NHRA, ASCS, Weekly

www.memphismotorsports.com

5500 Taylor Forge Drive

Millington, TN 38053

Tickets & Info: 901-358-7223 or 1-866-40-SPEED

TRACK FACTS

Distance: .75 miles

Degree of Banking in Turns: 11 degrees

Degree of Banking in Straights: 4 degrees

Shape: Oval

Camping & Tailgating: Memphis offers limited nonreserved and reserved track-side RV camping and parking. Prices vary depending on the event. For a complete listing of events and availability, call the ticket office. For more camping and RV camping, the Meeman-Shelby Forest State Park is located nearby. Ground fires are not permitted at the facility.

Michigan International Speedway

Called MIS by many, this facility is a huge hit with race fans. MIS offers racing from stock to open-wheel and has a full season of events. In the winter you can even catch some snowmobile action! The huge track offers campers and tailgaters a variety of camping options.

Series: NASCAR, BUSCH, INDY, WSA

www.mispeedway.com

12626 U.S. 12

Brooklyn, MI 49230

Tickets & Info 1-800-354-1010

TRACK FACTS

Distance: 2 miles

Degree of Banking in Turns: 18 degrees

Degree of Banking in Front Stretch: 12 degrees

Degree of Banking in Back Stretch: 5 degrees

Shape: D-shaped oval

Camping & Tailgating: MIS offers a huge selection of camping options, from a massive infield area to five outside camping areas. All within yards of the track. Normal track RV general camping rules apply. The ticket office can give you a complete list of rules, regulations and availability. There are several campgrounds within five miles or less of the track as well.

HEY RACE FANS, did you know that the first two-mile oval racetrack built in the United States was Michigan International Speedway?

The Milwaukee Mile

The name says it all. This one-mile track with low banking in the turns and even lower banking in the front and back stretches, offers fans great races.

Series: NASCAR, BUSCH, Craftsman, ARCA, INDY, ASA

www.milwaukeemile.com

7722 W. Greenfield Avenue

West Allis, WI 53214

Tickets & Info: 414-453-8277 or 1-800-955-5566

TRACK FACTS

Distance: 1 mile

Degree of Banking in Turns: 9.25 degrees

Degree of Banking in Straights: 2.5 degrees

Shape: Oval

Camping & Tailgating: RV parking is available about 300 yards from the track. For availability call the RV park office directly at (414) 266-7035. There is no tent camping allowed. All camping is located on the Milwaukee State Fairgrounds adjacent to the track. Visit their website at www.wistatefair.com.

Nashville Superspeedway

Like many of the other sights in the Nashville area, this place was built with fans in mind. Tons of great seating. Easy access in and out of the parking and camping areas. Pre-race concerts and more. The track is just east of Nashville in Lebanon, Tennessee.

Series: BUSCH, ARCA, NASCAR Elite, ARCA Truck, INDY

www.nashvillesuperspeedway.com

4847-F McCrary Road

Lebanon, TN 37090

Tickets & Info: 1-866-RACE-TIX

TRACK FACTS

Distance: 1.33 miles

Degree of Banking in Turns: 14 degrees

Degree of Banking in Front Stretch: 9 degrees

Degree of Banking in Back Stretch: 6 degrees

Shape: D-shaped oval

Track Surface: Concrete

Camping: RV camping on-site both reserved and nonreserved. Incredible views from the reserved bluff RV area. The campgrounds are all right next to the track. A great place to see a race and tailgate. Easy in and easy out!

New Hampshire International Speedway

Just over a mile, this track offers a true short track feel combined with some fairly high speeds along the fairly flat straightaways! That equals exciting racing. HUGE grandstands with great sight-lines make this a fan-friendly racetrack.

Series: NASCAR, BUSCH, ARCA, ASA, Craftsman, SCCA, WKA

www.nhis.com

1122 Route 106 North

Loudon, NH 03307

Tickets & Info: 603-783-4931

TRACK FACTS

Distance: 1.058 miles

Degree of Banking in Turns: 12 degrees

Degree of Banking in Straights: 2 degrees

Shape: D-shaped oval

Camping & Tailgating: New Hampshire offers RV camping on a reserved and first-come basis. All campers and RVs must be self-contained. Small wood or charcoal cooking fires are allowed if deemed that the area is safe and not in drought by the fire warden. So just plan on taking your gas grill. The camping areas are easy in and out, well lit and easy to get to and from the track. Golf carts, mopeds, or electric scooters are not allowed.

Phoenix International Raceway

When you head to Phoenix to see a race, make sure you are ready for a fun day at the track. This track has some great seating and many fan-friendly features. Lots of parking, RV areas and more.

Series: NASCAR, BUSCH, IRL, Grand Am

www.phoenixintlraceway.com

7602 S. Avondale Boulevard

Avondale, AZ 85323

Tickets & Info: 602-252-2227

TRACK FACTS

Distance: 1 mile

Degree of Banking in Turns 1 & 2: 11 degrees

Degree of Banking in Turns 3 & 4: 9 degrees

Degree of Banking in Front Stretch: 3 degrees

Degree of Banking in Back Stretch: 9 degrees

Shape: D-shaped oval

Camping & Tailgating: PIR offers RV camping. For information and availability about their schedule of events, call the ticket office.

Pikes Peak International Speedway

What else can you say? This is a great track located in a beautiful area of the country. A very fan-friendly place with plenty of room to expand seating, etc. The current grandstands offer some great sightlines of the track.

Series: BUSCH, AMA, USAC, IRL

www.ppir.com

16650 Midway Ranch Road

Fountain, CO 80817

Tickets & Info 1-888-306-7223

TRACK FACTS

Distance: 1 mile

Degree of Banking in Turns: 10 degrees

Degree of Banking in the front Stretch: 7 degrees

Degree of Banking in the Back Stretch: 3 degrees

Shape: Slight D-shaped oval

Camping & Tailgating: Pikes Peak offers some great trackside RV camping. Spots are limited, so call the ticket office for availability.

Pocono Raceway

Pocono has long been a fan favorite. The track offers three turns with different degrees of banking. A very fun racetrack design with clear sightlines throughout! They call it "the superspeedway that drives like a road course."

Series: NEXTEL, BUSCH, ARCA RE/MAX, SCCA

www.poconoraceway.com

P. O. Box 500

Long Pond, PA 18334-0500

Tickets & Info 1-800-RACEWAY

TRACK FACTS

Distance: 2.5 miles

Degree of Banking in Turns: 14 degrees, 8 degrees, 6 degrees

Shape: Tri-oval

Camping & Tailgating: Pocono is huge and offers camper and RV camping just about everywhere. The list of events and availability is something only the ticket office can handle. But you can find a good reserved spot just by calling the ticket office. There are several packages and prices to chose from. These include infield reserved, infield early bird, trackside, grandstand side and more.

The media is everywhere during race day. The Speed Channel catches up with driver Greg Biffle for a quick interview.

Richmond International Raceway

Fans love night races at Richmond! This classic short track always offers some fantastic racing no matter what series races there. TONS of great seats with fantastic views and many other fan-friendly features. This track started as a dirt track!

Series: NASCAR, BUSCH, ARCA, CRAFTSMAN, IRL

www.rir.com

P. O. Box 9257

Richmond, VA 23227

Tickets & Info: 1-866-455-RACE (7223)

TRACK FACTS

Distance: .75 miles

Degree of Banking in Turns: 14 degrees

Degree of Banking in Straights: 5 degrees

Shape: Oval

Camping & Tailgating: Call for availability; space is limited. Richmond offers full camper and RV camping. About the only restriction besides general safety rules is no ground fires, go-karts, golf carts or unauthorized vehicles.

Talladega Superspeedway

This is the track fans love and drivers worry about. I grew up with this track in the back of my mind because of it being close to my aunt and uncle's family lake house. In college I saw my first superspeedway race here. The fans bring tailgating to another level at Talladega. This track is over two miles long with short track banking and 4,000-feet-plus huge straightaways. WOW!

Series: NASCAR, BUSCH, ARCA, ASA

www.talladegasuperspeedway.com

3366 Speedway Blvd.

Talladega, AL 35160

Ticket Office Phone: 1-877-Go2-DEGA (462-3342)

TRACK FACTS

Distance: 2.66 miles

Degree of Banking in Turns: 33 degrees

Degree of Banking in Front Stretch: 18 degrees

Degree of Banking in Back Stretch: 2 degrees

Shape: Superspeedway D-shaped tri-oval—Yep, it is everything!

Camping: RV camping, camping on-site and nearby private camping. This is the place to be if you want to tailgate. Infield RV and camper and car parking are the things legends are made of.

HEY RACE FANS, did you know that according to Talladega Superspeedway officials, when NASCAR NEXTEL Cup race fans choose to stay on property during race weekends, the track becomes one of Alabama's largest cities for a weekend?

Texas Motor Speedway

Head to Texas for the longhorns and now for the racing! Texas Motor Speedway offers some great races that combine speedway speeds with short track turns. Toss in some great grandstands, wonderful foods in the concession stands and a fan-friendly environment, and you have a great place to watch a race. Located outside of Fort Worth, Texas.

Series: NASCAR, BUSCH, IRL

www.texasmotorspeedway.com

3545 Lone Star Circle

Justin, TX 76247

Tickets & Info: 1-817-215-8500

TRACK FACTS

Distance: 1.5 miles

Degree of Banking in Turns: 24 degrees

Degree of Banking in Dogleg: 5 degrees

Degree of Banking in Back Stretch: 5 degrees

Shape: Dogleg-shaped oval

Camping & Tailgating: Up to five options from high dollar RV reserved to the Lone Star Circle Tent City on NASCAR weekends. Texas offers up the world to RV campers and tailgaters. No open-pit fires are allowed, but charcoal and gas grills are.

Watkins Glen International

The Glen is one of the most famous road courses in the world. This track had humble beginnings when it started as a road course along the streets of Watkins Glen, New York. The original course combined ashpalt, cement and even dirt roads. Today when NASCAR hits the Glen, New York area fans pack the visitor-friendly track for great races.

www.theglen.com

2790 County Route 16

Watkins Glen International, NY 14891

Tickets & Info: 607-536-2481 or 607-535-2486

TRACK FACTS

Distance: 2.45 miles

Degree of Banking in Turns: Varies

Shape: Road course

Camping: The track offers a wide range of fan parking, tailgating and race-day events. Overnight parking is available, but call the ticket office for availability, dates, rules and regulations.

HEY RACE FANS, did you know that when Jeff Gordon captured his seventh road course victory at Watkins Glen in 2001, he made NASCAR history by setting a NASCAR Winston Cup record?

RACING FROM THE HEART

Everytime a driver races, a team enters a car or a fan walks through a gate, more than just a race is happening. In almost every racing series from Cup to your local dirt track, another side of the sport shines. In case you thought racing was just trading paint and hitting your points around the track, then you have to look again.

Today, almost every track, team, driver or series supports some sort of charity. It could be a local school, hospital or organization. Events could range from a driver's own golf tournament to elaborate fundraisers. The point is, the racing industry is one industry that knows how to give back to its fans and communities.

Here are only a few of the charities seen active in the Cup, BUSCH, ARCA, SAS, ASA and other racing series. There are plenty more! So keep your eyes . . . and pocketbooks open to help out your neighbor.

The Dale Jarrett Foundation

Dale Jarrett gives back to his community. Started in 2002, the foundation was set up to help charities around the Jarrett hometown area. But since then, they have grown to add more organizations to their list. The foundation is growing, and needs fan support. The Dale Jarrett Foundation helps support these and more charities: Brenner's Children's Hospital, the American Cancer Society and Project Potential. For more info, visit www.dalejarrettfoundation.org.

The Jeff Gordon Foundation

Not only has Jeff Gordon made a name for himself in the history books of racing, his name has also become one with many charities. The Jeff Gordon Foundation was set up in 1994. The foundation is not a stand-alone organization. Jeff was so helpful to so many needy charities that it only made sense to bring all of the support under one umbrella. The Jeff Gordon Foundation actually helps with several different charities such as the Make-A-Wish Foundation, the Marrow Foundation, a children's hospital and several more. Most are geared toward those charities that help very ill children. For more info, visit www.jeffgordonfoundation.org.

Kyle Petty Charity Ride

One of the most famous names in the industry is the Petty family. Kyle Petty and the rest of his family sponsor the Kyle Petty Charity Ride. The ride has actually grown into several motorcycle fundraising rides. All geared towards charities, the most famous is the ride for the Victory Junction Gang Camp. This original ride started in 1994 as just a growing group of riders and friends riding from North Carolina to Phoenix. As the number of riders grew, Petty formed the idea to raise money for charity. For more info, visit www.kylepettycharityride.com.

Morgan Shepherd Charitable Fund - Victory in Jesus

One of the nicer guys in the sport of racing, not only does Morgan Shepherd raise money to help people in the state of Virginia and other charities, but his whole race team is supported by a few sponsors and his great fans. Morgan Shepherd's Victory in Jesus race team tries to qualify at Cup events with tons of faith and a handful of donations to the Victory in Jesus team. For more info, visit www.morganshepherd.com.

Motor Racing Outreach

Founded in 1988, Motor Racing Outreach offers ministry services to several series including everything from NEXTEL Cup to powerboat racing. The idea behind MRO is simple. In a world where most people work during the traditional day of church, why not bring the wholesome church service and outreach to the track. For more info, visit www.waminc.org.

Ricky Craven Snowmobile Ride

One of the cooler charities going . . . pun not intended. The Ricky Craven Snowmobile Ride has been around for several years and has donated more than $1 million to several organizations including the Travis Roy Foundation, which helps spinal cord injury survivors. The RCSR also contributes to charities such as Make-A-Wish Foundation and Give Kids the World. For more info, visit www.rickycraven.com.

Speedway Charities / Speedway Children's Charities

This charity is known by many race fans. It has grown from a simple ball held by Bruton Smith to an organization that helps donate funds to many, many qualified charities. These include way too many organizations to list. If you have a particular cause and would like it to go to a charity near your hometown track, then visit the Speedway Children's Charities website. For more info, visit www.speedwaychar-ities.org.

Ward Burton Wildlife Foundation

When I spoke to Ward Burton about his foundation, you could tell it came from his heart. "I want to give back to my home and my friends, and help be a responsible steward for the land I love." You can't say it better than that. The foundation grew from Ward's early days as a child being dropped off for weekend camping trips in a rural cabin near his home. "I learned to love and respect the land." The foundation is set up to help educate children and others about our outdoors. For more info, visit www.twbwf.org.

Women's Auxiliary of Motorsports

The Women's Auxiliary of Motorsports is an organization whose members are made up of wives, mothers and sisters of drivers, team members, owners, sponsors and people in the racing world. WAM holds events such as golf tournaments to help raise money and awareness for charities such as the Victory Junction Gang, the Susan G. Komen Breast Cancer Foundation and Race Fans for a Cure. For more info, visit www.waminc.org.

a few more . . .

America Supports You • www.americasupportsyou.mil

Hendrick Motorsports Marrow Program
The Marrow Foundation • www.hendrickmotorsports.com

Michael Waltrip Operation Marathon
www.michaelwaltrip.com/marathon/

The Pit Board Charity • www.pitboardcharity.com

Race Against Drugs • www.raceagainstdrugs.org

St. Jude Children's Research Hospital • www.stjude.org

Terry Labonte Roam for a Home Foundation
www.roamforahome.org

As I said before, there are way too many charities to list. Some teams such as DEI, Hendrick Motorsports, Wood Brothers and more are well known for their work with charities. I suggest if you wish to back your favorite driver's or team's selected charity, then get on their website and look for a link to the organizations they support. It's a way you can do a good deed based around a great sport.

PROFILE INDEX

RECIPE INDEX

C

D

E

F

G

H

I

J

K

Q

R

Look for ***Checkered Flag Cooking*** and Kent's first coobook, ***Smoke in the Mountains***, in kitchen specialty stores, gift shops and bookstores, or order direct.

- Visit us on the web at **www.quailridge.com** and **www.thedeckchef.com.** While you're there, check out the free recipes, discount offers, other great books and so much more.
- Give us a call at **1-800-343-1583** to order with any major credit card.
- Mail the order form below with your check or money order to **Quail Ridge Press • P. O. Box 123 • Brandon, Mississippi 39043.**
- Or fax the order form below with your credit card information to **1-800-864-1082.**

Request a **FREE CATALOG** of all Quail Ridge Press cookbooks by calling **1-800-343-1583.**

ORDER FORM

Clip and Send to: QUAIL RIDGE PRESS • P. O. Box 123 • Brandon, MS 39043

❑ Check or money order enclosed

Charge to: ❑ Visa ❑ MasterCard ❑ American Express ❑ Discover

Card # __________ Expiration Date __________

Signature __________ Email Address __________

Name __________ Phone # __________

Address __________

City/State/Zip __________

	QUANTITY	PRICE	COST
Checkered Flag Cooking	______	@ $16.95 ea. =	______
Smoke in the Mountains Cookbook	______	@ $16.95 ea. =	______
		7% Tax for Mississippi residents	______
		Postage ($4.00 any number of books)	+ 4.00
		Total	______